AS Sociology

UNIT 1

AQA

Module 1: Families and Households

Joan Garrod

For Lillian

Philip Allan Updates
Market Place
Deddington
Oxfordshire
OX15 0SE

Orders

Bookpoint Ltd, 130 Milton Park, Abingdon, Oxfordshire, OX14 4SB
tel: 01235 827720
fax: 01235 400454
e-mail: uk.orders@bookpoint.co.uk
Lines are open 9.00 a.m.–5.00 p.m., Monday to Saturday, with a 24-hour message answering service. You can also order through the Philip Allan Updates website: www.philipallan.co.uk

ISBN-13: 978-0-86003-465-0
ISBN-10: 0-86003-465-8

This Guide has been written specifically to support students preparing for the AQA AS Sociology Unit 1 examination. The content has been neither approved nor endorsed by AQA and remains the sole responsibility of the author.

Printed by MPG Books, Bodmin

Philip Allan Updates' policy is to use papers that are natural, renewable and recyclable products and made from wood grown in sustainable forests. The logging and manufacturing processes conform to the environmental regulations of the country of origin.

AS Sociology

Contents

Introduction

■ ■ ■

Content Guidance

■ ■ ■

Questions and Answers

Introduction

About this guide

This unit guide is for students following the AQA AS Sociology course. It deals with the Module 1 topic **Families and Households**, which is examined within Unit 1. This topic is designed to give you a good understanding of the importance of the family both to individuals and to society as a whole. There are three sections to this guide:

- **Introduction** — this provides advice on how to use this unit guide, an explanation of the skills required in AS Sociology and suggestions for effective revision. It concludes with guidance on how to succeed in the unit test.

- **Content Guidance** — this provides an outline of what is included in the specification for Families and Households. It is designed to make you aware of what you should know before the unit test.

- **Questions and Answers** — this provides mock exam questions on Families and Households for you to try, together with some sample answers at grade-A and grade-C level. Examiner's comments are included on how the marks are awarded.

How to use the guide

To use this guide to your best advantage, you should refer to the Introduction and Content Guidance sections from the beginning of your study of Families and Households. However, in order to get full advantage from the Question and Answer section, you would be advised to wait until you have completed your study of the topic, as the questions are wide-ranging. When you are ready to use this section, you should take each question in turn, study it carefully, and either write a full answer yourself or, at the very least, answer parts (a) to (d) fully and write a plan for parts (e) and (f). When you have done this, study the grade-A candidate's answer and compare it with your own, paying close attention to the examiner's comments. You could also look at the grade-C answers and, using the examiner's comments as a guide, work out how to rewrite them to gain higher marks.

These tasks are quite intensive and time-consuming, and you should not be tempted to try to tackle all the questions in a short space of time. It is better to focus on one at a time, and spread the workload over several weeks — you can always find some time to do this, even while studying another topic. In addition to using the questions to consolidate your own knowledge and develop your exam skills, you should use at least some of the questions as revision practice — even just reading through the grade-A candidates' answers should provide you with useful revision material.

The AS specification

You will need to know and understand a range of relevant concepts and definitions, and be able to discuss the current situation regarding the diversity of types of family and household, as well as the changes that have occurred in these over the last 100 years or so. As well as being able to discuss a variety of studies on the family, you will need to know and understand the various sociological theories and perspectives on this important social institution — i.e. functionalist, Marxist, feminist, New Right and postmodern views. As with all modules in the specification, as well as displaying appropriate knowledge and understanding, you will need to show the ability to display a range of examinable skills, as outlined below.

The specification also requires you to understand what are known as 'core themes' in sociology. These are (a) socialisation, culture and identity, and (b) social differentiation, power and stratification. These themes have been incorporated into the content of each module, so if you do all the work you are set on this topic, you will have successfully covered the core themes, and there is no need for any extra work.

Examinable skills

There are two main examinable skills in the specification, also referred to as 'Assessment Objectives'. Each of these counts for half of the available marks, both within a question and in the AS qualification as a whole.

Assessment Objective 1 (AO1) is 'knowledge and understanding'. The skill of 'knowledge and understanding' is not quite as straightforward as it seems. You not only need to have sufficient 'knowledge' of the topic, you also need to show that you actually understand it, and are not just putting something down that you have learned by rote. Understanding, then, is shown by the way in which you select and use your knowledge to answer a particular question. It must be *relevant* knowledge, that is, appropriate to the question you are answering. You must also show that you have studied and understood a topic in a *sociological*, that is a specialist, way — covering sociological thought (particularly theories and perspectives), and sociological methods.

Assessment Objective 2 (AO2) covers 'identification, analysis, interpretation and evaluation'. In terms of how you display these skills in the exam, you must learn to:

- **identify** appropriate pieces of knowledge
- **distinguish** between facts and opinions
- **analyse** research methods and research studies in terms of their strengths and weaknesses
- **interpret** material such as research findings and statistics in order to identify any trends and uncover the (sometimes hidden) meanings
- and, perhaps most importantly of all, show the ability to **evaluate**

The skill of evaluation is an important one, and should be applied to all the material you come across during your study of the topic. In practice, this means that you should develop the habit of asking questions, such as 'Who says so?', 'How did they find that out?', 'Is there any other evidence of this?', 'Who does not agree with this view?', and so on. In perhaps more practical terms, it means that whenever you are introduced to a sociological perspective or study, you should find and learn at least two criticisms that have been made of it. You should also note, of course, which group or person has made these criticisms, as this is an important piece of information.

Study skills and revision strategies

Good preparation for revision actually starts the minute you begin to study sociology. One of the most important revision aids that you will have is your sociology folder, so it is important that you keep this in good order. Essentially, it should be divided into topic areas. It should contain all your class notes, handouts, notes you have made from textbooks, class and homework exercises and, of course, all your marked and returned work. If you are not by nature a neat and tidy person, you may find that you have to rewrite notes you make in class into a legible and coherent form before putting them in your folder. Be warned, though — this is something you should do straight away, as even after only a few days you will have forgotten things. If you keep a good folder throughout, reading through this will form a major part of your revision. In addition, you will, of course, need to re-read the relevant parts of your textbooks. Your own work also forms an important revision resource. Go back over your essays and exam answers, read your teacher's comments, and use these to see whether you can redo any pieces that did not score particularly good marks.

There is a wealth of statistical material on Families and Households available in reference books, such as *Social Trends* and *The British Social Attitudes Survey*, and also useful information in reports published by organisations such as The Family Policy Studies Centre, The Joseph Rowntree Foundation and various charities. Your school/college library and your local library will almost certainly contain a number of useful sources. Don't waste time hunting on your own — explain to the librarian what you are looking for, and ask for guidance. There are also a number of useful websites, and typing in key words and doing a search, or going to a specialist website, such as a national newspaper archive, will often produce helpful information. You should always remember, however, to check out the site carefully, to help determine the likely credibility of the information you download.

You should always write down the definition of a concept when you first come across it — it is a good idea to use a separate part of your folder for this purpose. In addition, it is useful to make a brief summary of research studies, particularly those not found within your textbook. Remember to include the title, author(s) and, most importantly, the date along with your summary of the method(s) used and the main findings. These should be kept in a section in your sociology folder, or you may wish to use a set of index cards for this purpose.

Another important aspect of revision is to practise writing answers within the appropriate time limit. Make sure you have sufficient time not only to complete all the parts of the question, but also to re-read your answer, in order to correct any silly mistakes that may have crept in while working under pressure.

Finally, you need to ensure that you have a thorough understanding of a range of appropriate concepts and studies. Again, this planned and comprehensive revision is not something that can be done the night before the exam — you should start at least a couple of weeks before the exam, and revise in concentrated bursts of time. People differ in this respect, but it is seldom a good idea to spend more than 2 hours at a time on revision, and for most people, two or three stints of an hour at a time spread out over a day or two will be more productive than a 2 or 3 hour session, particularly late at night.

The unit test

Families and Households is a Module 1 topic. This module also contains the topics of Health and Mass Media. The unit test will contain three questions, one on each of these three topics, and you will have to answer one question in the examination time of $1\frac{1}{4}$ hours. The unit as a whole is worth 35% of the AS qualification and $17\frac{1}{2}$% of the total A-level qualification. Each question is marked out of 60, and of the 60 marks, 30 are given to AO1 (knowledge and understanding) and 30 to AO2 (identification, analysis, interpretation and evaluation).

Each question in the examination will feature source material, or 'items' — usually two of them. These are designed to help you by providing information on which you may draw in your answer. It is therefore essential that before attempting to answer any part of the question, you read the items carefully, and continue to refer to them throughout the examination. Sometimes a question will make a specific reference to an item, such as 'With reference to Item A', or 'Using evidence from Item B and elsewhere'. In these cases you should make quite sure that you clearly follow the instruction. An easy way of doing this is to say, for example, 'The view referred to in Item A is that...', 'Item A shows evidence of...', 'Item B gives examples of...' or 'The view in Item B reflects the Marxist view of..., which has been criticised, particularly by functionalists, who argue that...'.

Each question is broken down into a number of parts, usually (a) to (f), each with its own mark allocation. The first series of questions, typically (a) to (d), will together add up to 20 marks, and require short answers. As is usual in such cases, the higher the mark allocation, the more you would normally need to write to gain full marks.

The remaining parts, (e) and (f), each carry 20 marks, and there is an important difference between them with regard to the balance of the two assessment objectives.

Part (e) is weighted towards knowledge and understanding, which carries 14 of the 20 available marks, leaving 6 marks for the remaining skills. This means that in answering this question, you should ensure that you show evidence of appropriate sociological knowledge and understanding. Remember, though, that 6 marks are for demonstration of the remaining skills, so these, particularly evaluation, should not be neglected. You should therefore make sure that you include some critical or evaluative comments at suitable points in your answer.

In part (f) the skills balance is reversed, that is, 14 of the 20 marks are awarded for the skills of identification, analysis, interpretation and evaluation, with 6 marks available for knowledge and understanding. As it is most unlikely that you would be able to demonstrate the AO2 skills without at the same time showing evidence of knowledge and understanding, your focus should be on showing sufficient evidence of the AO2 skills. You will be reminded of this by the wording of the question, which will usually ask you to 'assess' or 'evaluate' something.

Content
Guidance

This section is intended to show you the major issues, or topics, covered in **Families and Households**, together with a few key studies. Remember, though, that these are offered as guidance only — the list is neither exhaustive nor exclusive, that is, there are other concepts that are useful and many other studies that are relevant. With regard to studies, whatever textbook you use will contain sufficient examples for your needs, and your teacher will undoubtedly refer you to others. If you have back copies of *Sociology Review* or *S Magazine* in your library, you will also find a number of useful articles on this area of the course. In addition to 'studies', i.e. pieces of sociological research, there are other useful books and articles in which sociologists discuss their ideas about an aspect of the family. These will be referred to in your textbooks.

The content of Families and Households falls into four main areas:
- **the relationship of the family to the social structure**
- **changes in family and household structure**
- **changing patterns of marriage, cohabitation, separation, divorce and childbearing**
- **gender roles and domestic labour**

This section will first outline how these four main areas are included in the specification and will then go into further detail, discussing Marxist, functionalist, feminist, New Right and postmodern views of the topics.

Module content

What follows is a brief outline of what is included in the Families and Households topic of the Module 1 specification, i.e. the things that you should know before the unit test. It expands a little on the four content headings given for this topic in the specification.

Different views of the role of the family in society, and how those views may have changed over time

These cover Marxist, functionalist, feminist, New Right and postmodern views. You should be aware of differences within perspectives as well as between them. The views should be examined for similarities and differences regarding the following points.

- The main purpose/function of the family with regard to its benefits/shortcomings for society as a whole, different groups within society (e.g. the bourgeoisie, women) and individual family members.
- The relationship between the family and the economic structure of society, e.g. the family as a unit of production/consumption.
- How the role and structure of the family have been shaped/influenced by state policies and (an important point) how changes in the role and structure of the family have themselves influenced state policies.

What is meant by the terms 'families' and 'households', and the difference between them

- The structure of both families and households, i.e. their size and the relationships of members to each other, and how these have changed over time.
- The meaning of 'industrialisation' and 'urbanisation', and the relationship between each of these processes and families and households.
- The nature of the evidence regarding these relationships, for example: whether industrialisation brought about a shift from extended to nuclear families; whether before industrialisation people were living mainly in 'families' or 'households'; whether there were class/urban/rural differences; the situation today.

An understanding of how statistics on marriage, divorce, childbirth and cohabitation are presented, especially the notion of a 'rate'

- An outline knowledge of how each of these rates changed during the twentieth century, and especially over the last 50 years.
- The variety of reasons/explanations offered for each of these changes, for example: the relationship between changes in the laws on divorce and the divorce rate; reasons for the fall in the marriage rate; why in many cases 'cohabitation' may be viewed as just as stable a 'relationship' as marriage; reasons for the falling birth rate, particularly among some groups in society.
- The variation in types of family and household structure in contemporary Britain and whether these different types are linked to particular groups, for example age, regional, class, ethnic.

The meaning of 'roles' within the family, both between the adult partners and between adults and children

- The debate concerning the 'domestic division of labour' with regard to gender, and how the pattern of domestic work and childcare may be changing, and why.
- Economic and psychological power relationships in families, between adult partners and between adults and children, for example who controls the finances, who makes what kinds of decisions, and issues of physical and emotional abuse.
- The idea of 'childhood' as a biological, social and legal construct.
- Changes in the status and rights of children.

In addition to this specific knowledge and understanding of Families and Households, you should also recognise how the topic addresses the two core themes of (a) Socialisation, Culture and Identity, and (b) Power, Differentiation and Stratification. This would include the following:

- The family as the main agency of the primary socialisation of children; teaching them the language, norms and values of the society.
- Cultural differences within different family groups, based on age, region, social class, religion and ethnicity.
- Family roles as an important source of identity, for example mother, father, husband, wife, son, daughter, grandmother, daughter-in-law, grandson etc.
- Power differences in the family, based on gender, age, religious beliefs etc.
- The differentiation of family structures in society.
- The effects of stratification in society on families, for example in terms of wealth and income, health, housing etc.

Those of you who hope to continue your study of sociology into the second year, to take the A-level qualification, should also develop an awareness of how aspects of Families and Households link to the synoptic topics of Crime and Deviance and Stratification. Links to Stratification have already been mentioned above, and your teacher will help you to identify links with the topic of Crime and Deviance. These will include New Right views on the relationship between family structure and 'social problems', such as certain types of criminal and deviant behaviour, domestic and other types of abuse in families as examples of deviant behaviour, links between social class and crime, socialisation into 'antisocial' norms and behaviour, and so on. Note that many of these links reflect certain views, and should be treated as critically as any other information you come across in your study of this subject.

For the purposes of guidance, each of the four sub-sections that follow relates to one of the four content area headings for this topic set out in the specification.

Relationship of the family to the social structure

The role of the family in society

Functionalist views

- Murdock argued that the family is a universal institution, that is, it exists in one form or another in all societies.
- Families are essential to the survival of a society as they perform certain vital functions. These include: the economic function (providing food and shelter, acting as work units to make or grow things); the sexual/reproduction function (providing socially acceptable ways of regulating sexual behaviour and producing the next generation); and the socialisation function (providing the primary socialisation that enables children to learn the norms and values of their society and to behave in socially approved ways).
- Parsons believed that in modern societies some of these functions disappear or are eroded, and argued that there are two 'basic and irreducible functions', namely the primary socialisation of children and the stabilisation of the adult personality.

Evaluation

- The functionalist view emphasises the positive role of the family, and neglects the 'darker' side of family life and the way in which it does not necessarily benefit all individuals.
- It fails to recognise the wide diversity of family and kinship structures and, particularly in the case of Parsons, places undue emphasis on the small, isolated nuclear family, typical of the white American middle class.
- It does not acknowledge alternatives to the family.

Key concepts

needs of society; universality of the family; functions of the family; primary socialisation

Marxist views

- The family is not an institution of benefit to society as a whole, but rather serves the interests of the powerful in society.
- In industrial societies, the family helps to service and maintain the economic system of capitalism which is the basis of the power of the bourgeoisie.
- There are other ways of fulfilling the tasks currently performed by families.
- The family in capitalist society is an institution that particularly oppresses women.

Evaluation

- Marxist views are guilty of 'economic determinism', that is, they see the nature of the family as stemming from the 'needs' of a particular economic system, such as capitalism.
- By focusing on the negative and exploitative aspects of the family, they fail to acknowledge the benefits of the family to society and to individuals.

Key concepts

capitalism; capitalist society; bourgeoisie; economic determinism

Feminist views

Note that there are different types of feminism, and that different groups have different ideas. You should be able to mention two or three different kinds of feminist view — the statements below are general ones.

- The family is a patriarchal institution that serves the interests of men and exploits women.
- The family has an ideological role in society — a particular type of family structure, the two-parent nuclear family, is presented as the 'ideal'.
- Roles within the family are not 'natural' but are socially constructed.

Evaluation

- Many feminist writers fail to take account of the variations in family structure and roles, and assume that all women are equally exploited within the family.
- There is a neglect of the positive side of family life, particularly for women.

Key concepts

patriarchy; patriarchal society; ideological role; socially constructed roles

New Right views

These views are frequently expressed by non-sociologists, and not backed by empirical evidence, but are often influential in shaping both public opinion and government policies.

- The traditional nuclear family is the 'cornerstone of society'.
- The decline of both traditional family values and the traditional family structure is a major contributor to various 'social problems', particularly crime, high spending on welfare benefits, educational underachievement and the existence of a socially undesirable 'underclass'.

Evaluation

- New Right views are often more 'political' than sociological, and are not backed by empirical evidence.
- Many features blamed on the decline of the traditional family and traditional family values, such as family breakdown, child poverty and educational underachievement, are the result of inadequate social policies and the pervasive inequality within society.
- There is no evidence that the 'traditional family values' to which reference is so

often made were ever universally accepted. Historical evidence shows that family breakdown, crime, poverty, domestic violence and lone-parent families are not new features of society.

Key concepts

traditional family values; underclass

Postmodern views

- No one type of family structure should be considered as more desirable than others. Rather, individuals should choose the type of family and the role(s) they play within that family according to their view of what is best for them.
- Following from this, 'alternative' family structures, such as lone-parent households and single-sex couples, and features such as serial relationships, childlessness by choice and a high divorce rate should not be viewed as 'problematic' or 'undesirable'.
- It can be argued that the traditional two-parent family is actually undesirable, as it is a powerful force in the construction of gender identities which can work to the disadvantage of both men and women.

Evaluation

- Too much freedom and individual choice can be detrimental both to individuals and to society.
- A certain degree of structure and the acceptance of certain role obligations are necessary for the maintenance and stability of society.

Key concepts

postmodern society; individual choice; the social construction of gender

The family and the economic structure

Functionalist views

- All institutions in society serve to meet the 'needs' of that society.
- The dominant structure of the family will be that which best meets the 'needs' of the economy at that time.
- There is a relationship between the different parts and institutions in society, so that a change in one will lead to a change in another.
- As a society moves from being predominantly rural and agricultural to predominantly urban and industrial, there is a need for a change in family structure, as the needs of the economy have changed.
- Rural and agricultural societies are best served by extended family structures, where families form work groups and where kin can support each other.
- Urban and industrial societies are best served by people living in small nuclear families, where traditional notions of ascribed status and elders as 'family leaders'

no longer exist, and where family members are geographically mobile and can easily move to where they are needed to work in new centres of production. In such families, there would be a male breadwinner with female and child dependants.

Evaluation

– The functionalist view is not supported by empirical evidence, which shows that both in the past and at present, society is characterised by a variety of family structures.
– The main move towards the smaller nuclear family of today did not occur until the early twentieth century, and even then 'pockets' of the more traditional structures remained.

Key concepts

industrialisation; urbanisation; extended family; nuclear family; economic needs; functions of the family; geographical mobility

Marxist and Marxist/feminist views

- The dominant structure of the family at any time will be that which best meets the needs of capitalism and therefore benefits the bourgeoisie.
- The nuclear family with a male breadwinner supported by the free domestic labour of his wife, who also raises the next generation of workers, best suits the needs of industrial capitalism.
- If wives were paid for their domestic labour, this would be a huge cost to employers.
- Women also form an important 'reserve army of labour', working for nothing in the home when they are not needed in the workforce, but capable of being drawn into the workforce when necessary.
- The need of the male breadwinner to provide financial support for his family reduces his ability to take industrial action by withdrawing his labour.
- Wives provide important emotional support to their partners, helping them to cope better with the strains and frustration of work in a capitalist system.
- Family roles, based on the authority of the father/parents, teach children to submit passively to authority, which is a desirable attribute of a capitalist workforce.
- The family is an important unit of consumption.

Evaluation

– Marxist and Marxist/feminist views fail to take account of differences in family roles and structures.
– They are guilty of 'economic determinism', i.e. suggesting that the underlying economic structure determines the structure of the family.

Key concepts

capitalism; bourgeoisie; reserve army of labour; patriarchy; domestic labour; the ideological role of the family

The family and state policies

You should have some knowledge of current and recent social policies on the family. In particular, you should be aware that some sociologists, particularly feminists, believe that social policies on the family reflect an ideological view that actively tries to promote a particular type of family structure, namely that of the nuclear family. The idea that one particular type of family is promoted in this way is referred to as 'the ideology of familism'. When you consider various social policies, you should consider whether they do, in fact, appear actively to promote the two-parent nuclear family.

The New Right view is that certain social policies (e.g. providing benefits for single mothers, and making divorce easier) undermine the traditional family structure and contribute to 'social problems'.

You will find helpful details of social policies on the family and other research on various aspects of the family on the government website (**http://open.gov.uk/** — once in the site, look up 'Family Policy Unit'). You can also find useful information on the website of the Family Policy Studies Centre (**http://www.fpsc.org.uk**).

Key concepts

the ideology of familism; ideological state apparatus; traditional family values; family-friendly policies; the nanny state; the underclass

Changes in family and household structure

The following are some of the more important changes in family and household structure. For many of these changes, you will find supporting statistical evidence in recent editions of *Social Trends*.

- A shift towards smaller, more isolated, nuclear families with less face-to-face contact with kin. There are, however, some important ethnic differences in this respect, with many families from the Indian subcontinent and those of Cypriot origin keeping very close contact with the wider family. Again, it is important to know how 'contact' is being measured. While it is true that members of some families do not have a great deal of face-to-face contact with kin, links are maintained in other ways, for example by visiting, telephoning, sending e-mails, etc. It is therefore unwise to suggest that 'the extended family' is disappearing, although we may need to refine our definition of this.
- A significant growth in the number and percentage of families headed by lone parents (the overwhelming majority of whom are women), now comprising

almost one in four of all families with dependent children. Over one in five of all dependent children now live in a family headed by a single parent. The two most common reasons for heading a lone-parent family are 'single lone motherhood' (never-married, non-cohabiting women with children), and divorce or separation. Reasons offered for the growth in lone-parent families, apart from the incidence of separation and divorce, include the availability of welfare benefits, the high rate of teenage pregnancies in Britain, and changing social norms resulting in a decrease in the stigmatisation of being a lone parent, particularly an unmarried mother.

- A rise in single-person households, currently comprising almost 30% of all households. Of these one-person households, almost half consist of a person under pensionable age. Reasons for this pattern are the growth of 'young singletons', including young people who may be in a relationship but who choose to live alone, and the rise in the number of divorced or separated people who have not formed another co-residential partnership. In addition, the increase in life expectancy has added to the number of elderly widowed people living alone.
- An increase in the number of 'empty-nest' families as children grow up and leave the family while the parents are still relatively young. This is also coupled to the rise in life expectancy.
- Note that there remain some important differences in family and household structures based on class, age, religion, region and ethnicity.

Key concepts

family; household; kin; isolated nuclear family; extended family; lone-parent families; life expectancy

Changing patterns of marriage, cohabitation, separation, divorce and childbearing

You should be aware of the following important changes and their link to changes in family and household structure. You should also be able to discuss the different views on both the causes and the consequences of these changes.

- A growth in 'reconstituted' families following divorce and remarriage. More than two in five of all marriages involve the remarriage of at least one partner, and a growing number of children live with a step-parent.
- A fall in the marriage rate, and a growth in cohabitation. Although marriage is still the usual form of partnership between men and women, the number of marriages has declined substantially since a peak in 1970. Currently, roughly a quarter of all

non-married men and women between the ages of 16–59 are cohabiting at any one time. Cohabitation is, of course, often followed by marriage.

- An increase in divorce following various legal changes, particularly the implementation in 1971 of the Divorce Reform Act. The increase in the number of divorces appears to have levelled off, partly at least reflecting the fall in the number of marriages. Increasingly, women are the petitioners for divorce, and about seven of every ten divorce decrees granted are to women. Reasons offered for the increase in divorce include: the legal changes making it easier for divorces to be granted; changing social attitudes (at least partly a result of the growing incidence of divorce); growing expectations of marriage for both men and women; the influence of feminist ideas (particularly that of women's rights to personal happiness and fulfilment within marriage); the isolation of the nuclear family from a geographically close supportive network of kin; and the growing pressures faced by many couples (including money problems and long hours at work).

- A fall in the fertility rate, leading to smaller families and a growth in childless couples. There are currently fewer than 60 births per 1000 women of child-bearing age per year, compared with 115 at the start of the twentieth century. In the 1970s, fertility fell below the rate to keep the population size stable (this ignores the effects of migration), and has remained below this level ever since. There has been a recent increase in the average age of women at the time of their first birth, with women aged 25–29 the most likely to give birth for the first time, and women aged 30–34 now more likely to give birth to their first child than women aged 20–24. A growing number of couples choose to remain childless. Reasons for the fall in fertility rates and the increase in the average age of motherhood include: the fall in the infant mortality rate; the greater availability and choice of reliable contraception; later marriage; the high cost of raising children; medical improvements in childbirth; the increase in the proportion of women in higher education; more employment opportunities for women leading to an increased proportion in the labour market; and changes in women's perceptions of their role.

Key concepts

marriage rate; divorce rate; fertility rate; infant mortality rate; cohabitation; social norms; serial monogamy

Gender roles and domestic labour

Evidence still points to the fact that, despite often being breadwinners, women spend more time on, and take more responsibility for, domestic work and childcare than their male partners. Many feminists attribute this to the existence of patriarchy and the resulting socialisation of males and females into a belief that domestic work and childcare is a 'natural', or at least socially approved and desirable, primary role for women.

Parsons and Bales, from a functionalist viewpoint, argued that in the conventional (and desirable) nuclear family there are two complementary roles for the adult partners. The male plays the 'instrumental' role of breadwinner and provider, and has the main contacts with the outside world through his employment, while the female plays the 'expressive' role of nurturer and homemaker. According to Parsons and Bales, these roles are based on the biological and evolutionary differences between males and females, and together provide the most suitable conditions for a stable family life and the primary socialisation of children.

In 1975, Young and Willmott argued that families were becoming, and would continue to become, more 'symmetrical', that is, the roles played by men and women within the family would become more 'equal'.

A number of feminist sociologists, notably Ann Oakley, conducted research that cast doubt on this view, showing that housewives continue to bear the main burden of housework and childcare.

Key concepts

symmetrical family; instrumental and expressive role; joint/segregated conjugal roles; women's dual role; women's triple shift; emotion work

Children and childhood

- The social construction of childhood — the ways in which 'childhood' is not a simple question of biological/physiological maturity, but reflects views regarding the attitudes towards and appropriate treatment of those defined as 'children'. How our notions of 'childhood' have shown considerable changes over time.
- The development of the 'child-centred family'.
- Changes in the legal rights and status of children, with regard to employment, education, physical abuse and criminal behaviour, and how these are linked to the prevailing views of children and 'childhood'.
- The suggested 'loss of innocence' of childhood as, via the mass media, children increasingly have access to formerly 'adult' material on issues such as death and sex.
- The alleged exploitation of children by advertisers, as they are seen as an important consumer group for a wide range of goods.

Key concepts

the social construction of childhood

Questions
&
Answers

This section of the guide provides you with six questions on the topic of **Families and Households** in the style of the AQA unit test. The first five questions are followed by a grade-A candidate response. It is important to note that these are not 'model answers' — they do not represent the only, or even necessarily the best, way of answering these questions. It would be quite possible, particularly in the answers to (e) and (f), to take a different approach, or to use different material, or even to come to a different conclusion, and still gain very high marks. Rather, the answers represent a particular 'style': one that answers the question set and displays the appropriate skills, including using suitable concepts and studies, displaying a critical and evaluative awareness towards the material used, and presenting a logically structured argument. Three of the questions also have a grade-C candidate answer that is basically on the right track, but which fails, for various reasons, to score very high marks.

A sixth question is provided which is not accompanied by a student answer, but is left for you to write your own. Again, some pointers are given to help put you on the right track.

Examiner's comments
The candidate answers are accompanied by examiner's comments. These are preceded by the icon ℮ and indicate where credit is due. For the grade-A answers, the examiner shows you what it is that enables the candidates to score so highly. Particular attention is given to the candidates' use of the examinable skills: knowledge and understanding, and analysis and evaluation. For the grade-C answers, the examiner points out areas for improvement, specific problems and common errors. You are also invited to rewrite the answer in order to gain higher marks, and some pointers are given to show you how you might do this.

Family structure; feminist views on the family; the family and ideology

Item A

The average household size in Great Britain had been about 4.6 people for many years until the early twentieth century. Since then it has almost halved, to 2.4 people per household in 1998–99, as the number of households has grown at a faster rate than the population. Trends towards smaller families, and more people living alone, help to explain this increase in the number of households.

One-person households have increased particularly rapidly. In 1901 about one in 20 households in Great Britain comprised one person living alone; this had increased to just under one in three by 1998–99. Since the early 1960s there has also been a decline in the proportion of 'traditional' households consisting of a couple with dependent children. In 1961, 38% of households in Great Britain were of this type, but by 1998–99 this had decreased to 23%.

Source: adapted from *Social Trends*, No. 30, 2000.

Item B

Many feminist sociologists have been keen to note that our common-sense under-standing of the family is often at odds with the reality of family life for many. This focus on 'common sense' is known in the sociological literature as an ideological view of the family and is seen to be present in functionalist theory, in the ideas of many politicians — including the New Right and maybe even the New Left — and displayed through the media.

The ideology of the family in contemporary life takes for granted the fact that we should all 'need' and 'want' a nuclear family. This is the 'cornflake packet' approach to the family — the idea that this sort of romanticised, happy 'safe haven' of the nuclear family only exists ideologically in the media and especially in television advertisements.

Source: Warren Kidd (1999) 'Family diversity in an uncertain future', *Sociology Review*, Vol. 9, No. 1.

(a) **Explain what is meant by a household (Item A).** (2 marks)
(b) **Suggest *two* explanations for the trend towards smaller families.** (4 marks)
(c) **Identify *three* reasons for the increase in one-person households.** (6 marks)
(d) **Identify and briefly explain *two* reasons why functionalist sociologists have emphasised the importance of the 'traditional nuclear family'.** (8 marks)

question

(e) **Examine the claim made by some feminist sociologists that marriage and family life can be disadvantageous to women.** (20 marks)

(f) **Using material from Item B and elsewhere, assess the view that the media and some politicians present an ideological view of the family.** (20 marks)

Total: 60 marks

■ ■ ■

Answer to question 1: grade-A candidate

(a) One person living alone or a group of people, related or not, living at the same address and sharing the accommodation and some meals together.

> *⊘* This gets across the important point that a household can consist of a single person, and that the people forming the household may or may not be related. Thus, most families form a household, but not all households are composed of families. (2 out of 2 marks)

(b) There are more lone-parent families, with just one adult and children.
There is reliable contraception, for example the pill, so families are more able to control the number of children they have.

> *⊘* Both these explanations are correct, so the candidate gains the maximum 4 marks. Other suitable explanations would be the fact that the fall in the infant mortality rate means that parents now expect all their children to survive; couples are having fewer children because of the expense of bringing up children; and more women are in paid employment.

(c) Young people now often live alone in their own home before marriage or cohabitation.
People who have divorced or whose relationship has broken up will often live alone, especially if they are men, because the children of divorced parents will tend to live with the mother.
There is an increase in the number of elderly widowed people.

> *⊘* The three main reasons are correctly identified, for the maximum 6 marks. Another possible explanation is the number of people who have come to Britain on a temporary basis to work, and who have taken up residence for a period, often in rented accommodation.

(d) Functionalists believe that the roles of husband and wife are complementary, with the husband taking the providing role (instrumental) and the wife taking the caring/nurturing role (expressive). These roles are best played out in the nuclear family.
They also believe that the traditional nuclear family provides the best method of carrying out the primary socialisation of the children, as the children have two different adult role models to learn from.

📝 Two correct reasons identified, so 2 marks for each, and an additional 2 marks for each of the two brief explanations, giving the candidate the maximum **8 marks**. Other reasons could include Parsons's view of the 'stabilisation of the adult personality' within the nuclear family, or the socially approved and controlled satisfaction of sexual needs.

(e) A number of feminist sociologists, including Oakley, Ansley, Delphy and Leonard, have pointed to the number of ways that women are disadvantaged in the family, especially as a wife and mother. Feminists believe that we live in a patriarchal society, that is, a society where men have most of the power, and this gives men power in all situations, including within the family.

📝 A strong start, which includes the names of some relevant feminist sociologists, showing a good understanding of the question. The important concept of 'patriarchal society' is introduced, with an explanation showing that it is clearly understood.

In Victorian days, women had even less power than today, and could barely exist outside of the control of a man, first their father and then their husband. At one time they couldn't own property in their own right, and they didn't get the vote or the right to divorce until long after such rights were given to men.

📝 A short historical note, showing that the disadvantages experienced by women are not new. Fortunately, this part was kept very brief, and avoided the tendency to go on at length about something that is only marginally relevant to the question. Unless a historical perspective is obviously required by the question, it is better to stick to contemporary issues and material. If historical material is included, keep it short and make sure it is relevant to the question.

Although this is no longer the case, the feminist argument is that women are still exploited within the family. Oakley's research showed the unequal division of domestic labour within a household, and much more recent studies than hers have shown that, in spite of most women now having paid employment, they still spend much longer on housework and childcare than their partners. Being a wife/mother and a worker leads to a 'dual role' for women in the family, but Dunscombe and Marsden have gone further and said that we should also add in the caring and nurturing role (what Ansley has called being the 'takers of shit') and therefore women can be said to have a 'triple shift'.

📝 The answer is neatly brought back to the present by the phrase 'although this is no longer the case', and by pointing out that feminists believe that exploitation is still taking place. Oakley's study is used well, the main point being made without spending time describing the study in detail, and with an important comment showing understanding of the fact that it is now quite dated. There is some good use of relevant concepts — 'division of domestic labour', 'dual role' and 'triple shift' — together with further reference to relevant sociologists.

Exploitation at work means that most women earn less than men, but even when they are a big contributor to the household finances, their earnings are often seen as supplementing the man's, with the man still being seen as the main bread-winner. Taking the time out to have babies and look after them, at least for a while, also has a bad effect on women's careers, putting them way behind men in the promotion stakes. Women with young children often have to fit their work around childcare commitments, leading many of them into having to work part-time. Also, men still tend to take the major decisions in a family. For example, it is usually the man's job that decides where the family will live.

✎ The reference to work and women's earnings is tied closely to the question of women's disadvantages arising from the family, avoiding the danger of going off the point and simply talking about unequal pay at work. The issue of male power in decision-making is also raised, though not pursued.

Lastly, studies have shown that married women have poorer health than single women, probably as a result of all the extra work they do, and the strain of having to be the comforter and supporter of all the other members of the family. There is also the sad fact that many women are the victims of domestic violence, and recent reports show that this is actually on the increase.

✎ A further area of disadvantage is raised, that of health, with some suggestions to explain why this should be so. Reference is also made to the important issue of domestic violence, and knowledge shown of recent information on this topic.

However, while feminists raise some very important issues, family life isn't all bad news for women. Many women get great satisfaction from being a wife and mother, and many will have a more comfortable lifestyle living as a couple, especially if they are both earners, than they would on their own, although this is just as true for men. It is also true that there has been some movement, at least in some groups of society, towards the men taking a greater share in domestic work and childcare, even though it is not yet equal. Overall, though, the feminists and their research make out a strong case for the fact that marriage and family life can be disadvantageous to women.

✎ The answer is brought to a conclusion with some evaluation of the debate, including bringing in some information to act as a kind of counter-balance to the feminist arguments and the evidence that has previously been discussed. The answer is concluded with a reference back to the original question.

✎ **Overall, this is a very good answer which stays firmly focused on the question and shows a good knowledge and understanding of the topic. Good use is made of relevant sociological concepts, and there are appropriate references to feminist sociologists. Some reference could have been made to different types of feminism. The answer is quite long, and some students might find that they are unable to write as much as this in the time provided. A shorter answer could leave out the 'historical' paragraph, and perhaps use**

only one of the examples showing the adverse effects on women's employment of being a mother. The skills balance for this question is 14 marks for knowledge and understanding and 6 marks for analysis and evaluation. The answer shows good evidence of both these skills and scores 18 out of the 20 marks available.

(f) According to Item B, there is a view of family life put across by the media and some politicians that is not 'real', but is a romanticised view of how some people believe that families ought to be. This view is sometimes referred to as the 'cornflake packet' or 'cereal packet' family. This is because advertising for certain products consumed by families often shows a certain type of family — white, middle-class, a mum and a dad and two smiling children, usually a boy and a girl. This ignores the fact that many people live in lone-parent families, many people are members of ethnic minorities, many couples do not have children and some people live in gay-couple relationships — even, in a few cases, with children.

> The opening paragraph 'unpacks' the question and shows a good understanding of the concept of the 'cornflake packet' family. Evaluation is shown by pointing out groups that do not fit this image.

Again, for many people, family life is not as warm and cosy as the image suggests. Many families live in poverty, and some family members suffer abuse, both physical and psychological, at the hands of other members of their families, such as abused children and women with violent partners. This has been pointed out by feminist sociologists in particular, and is supported by crime figures.

> Another aspect of family life mentioned in Item B is addressed here, namely that of the family as a 'safe haven', and evaluation is shown again by pointing to examples where this is not the case.

Item B also says that this ideological view of the family is shown in the ideas of some politicians. There is evidence for this, as certain government policies from both Labour and the Conservatives seem to benefit a particular type of family, such as the married couple tax allowance and some of the current 'family-friendly' policies. Politicians from the so-called 'New Right' are convinced that social problems such as crime and delinquency, truancy from school and even football hooliganism arise because of the number of people not brought up in conventional two-parent families, with the mother staying at home to look after the children and the father being the breadwinner.

> The issue of the views of politicians is addressed, with supporting evidence in favour of the view expressed in Item B.

Various reasons have been put forward as to why some groups should present an ideological view of the family. Marxists would argue that it is because the traditional nuclear family is the structure best suited to capitalism, with the male worker being cared for and nurtured at no charge by the woman, who also raises the next generation of workers and cares for them. Women are supposed, in this view,

to form a reserve army of labour, ready to come out of the family and be a worker if the capitalist economy needs more workers, as happened in both World Wars. Feminists would argue that the ideological view of the family, in which the woman is the lesser partner in terms of power and earnings, and is the one responsible for housework and childcare, is the type of family best suited to a patriarchal system, where it benefits men.

A useful paragraph that brings in two important perspectives on the family and uses them to discuss the view expressed in the essay title.

However, is it true to say that the 'cornflake packet' images of the family are the only ones that we receive from the media and politicians? While it used to be the case that many sitcoms did show this stereotypical picture of family life, this is no longer true. All the major soaps such as *EastEnders*, *Coronation Street*, *Brookside*, etc. show different types of families with a range of problems — divorce, births outside marriage, affairs, rape, domestic violence and even murder. As many people watch these programmes, they are certainly getting an alternative view of family life to the 'cornflake packet'. It is not only in soaps that these images occur. Some drama programmes show other types of relationship, such as *Queer as Folk* and *Rhona*. The newspapers also deal with a range of issues and family problems; in fact, they seem to think that these are really newsworthy, while living in a conventional family is dull and uninteresting.

Knowledge, understanding and evaluation are shown by a brief discussion of media programmes and stories that do not present the ideological view of the family expressed in Item B.

Also, many politicians do not preach the benefits of the 'cornflake packet' family. While Tony Blair is held up as the model family man, other politicians live in less conventional families; they have affairs, are divorced, and some are openly gay. Even Tony Blair has a wife with a high-powered job, and took paternity leave when his last baby was born, which goes partly against the stereotype. Some of the 'family-friendly' policies are also aimed at other types of family, such as lone-parent families, for example, helping lone mothers to train and get back to work.

The logical structure of the answer is again shown by presenting evidence against the view expressed in Item B, this time concerning politicians, and again showing evidence of both skills.

Therefore, while some politicians and certain types of media, especially some advertisements, do present an ideological view of the family, there is also evidence that other views of the family are regularly presented.

A brief but relevant conclusion which summarises the main argument of the answer.

Overall, this is a very good and detailed answer that stays firmly focused on the question and shows evidence of both skills. In part (f), 14 of the 20 marks

are given for analysis and evaluation. Here, the candidate shows good evidence of these skills by analysing and assessing the extent to which the view expressed in the question is borne out by the evidence. It is also important that the answer addresses both 'the media' and 'some politicians', as required by the question. For (f), therefore, the candidate scores 20 out of 20 marks.

Again, the answer is quite long, and some students would have difficulty in producing an answer of this length in the time provided. Have a look at both (e) and (f) and see how, without altering the basic structure, you could make the answers a little shorter. The best way to do this is probably to look at the examples given, and see whether these could be reduced in some way. Remember the different skills-balance of the two questions, however, and make sure that (e) has sufficient knowledge and understanding, and (f) sufficient analysis and evaluation to score well.

Divorce; feminist contributions to the study of the family

Item A

A period of unprecedented change in British family life, where adults lead more isolated lives, bringing up children on their own or not having them at all, is described in a report by the independent Family Policy Studies Centre. The report paints a picture of an evolving society with fewer children, fewer marriages, more divorces and more solo living, where 'marriage and partnerships are much more fragile than they were'.

21% of dependent children now live in lone-parent households (the vast majority with their mother), compared with 7% in 1972. The number of lone parents has trebled in the past 25 years — there were about 1.6 million such parents by the mid-1990s. Within that 1.6 million, the fastest growing group is single, never-married, lone mothers. Their proportion, 42% in 1997, is nearly double the proportion of 24% for 1984.

The annual marriage rate is at its lowest level since records began 160 years ago. Of every five marriages, two will end in divorce. But marriage is still more stable than cohabitation, with couples who live together unmarried three or four times more likely to split up.

Source: adapted from Will Woodward (2000) 'Are we turning into a nation of loners?', the *Guardian*, 27 March.

Item B

There can be little doubt that developments in feminist thought and practice have had a major influence upon the study of the family. In the first place, and most crucially, they have stressed that gender is a major feature of family living. Feminists argue that it should be recognised that families contain both men and women and that gender often has a profound impact on the ways in which individuals actually experience and understand living in families. Moreover, such differences are not to be seen simply as differences but also as inequalities. Feminists argue that, for example, violence against wives is not simply a matter of individual, and possibly abnormal, psychology, but is shaped by patterns of inequality between men and women both within the family and within the wider society.

Source: adapted from David Morgan (1987) 'Sociology, society and the family', *Social Studies Review*, Vol. 2, No. 5.

(a) Explain what is meant by the 'marriage rate' (Item A). (2 marks)

(b) Suggest *two* reasons why the number of lone-parent families has risen in the last 25 years. (4 marks)

(c) Identify *three* 'inequalities' that may exist between men and women in families. (6 marks)

(d) Identify and explain *two* reasons for the rise in the divorce rate since 1970. (8 marks)

(e) Outline the arguments and evidence for the view that a rise in the divorce rate does not necessarily mean that people are disenchanted with the institution of marriage. (20 marks)

(f) Using material from Item B and elsewhere, assess the contribution made by feminist sociologists to the study of the family. (20 marks)

Total: 60 marks

■ ■ ■

Answer to question 2: grade-C candidate

(a) How many marriages take place each year.

> ☑ This implies a 'number' rather than a 'rate', i.e. so many per thousand, and therefore scores no marks.

(b) Rising divorce. A lot of people don't bother to get married, but cohabit instead.

> ☑ The first answer is too brief to allow the examiner to know for sure what the student is thinking. It is true that the increase in divorce is a factor in the growth of lone-parent families, but of course only in families where there are dependent children who are left to live with just one of their parents. In this case the student is given the benefit of the doubt, but this answer shows that it is always safer to make your meaning explicit. The second answer gains no marks, as cohabiting couples with dependent children are not classified as 'lone-parent families'. Overall the candidate scores 2 out of 4 marks.

(c) The man has more power. The man is the 'boss' of the family. The woman does more housework than the man.

> ☑ This answer shows that even in short-answer questions it is important to write enough to make your meaning quite clear. In this answer, saying that the man has 'more power' and is 'the boss' of the family is really saying the same thing in a different way, so it is not possible to award marks for both answers. The third answer gains 2 marks, giving the candidate 4 out of 6 marks for this answer. Rewrite the first answer so that the meaning is made quite clear, and think of a third 'inequality' that would gain 2 marks.

(d) The spread of feminist views and women's lib, so women nowadays won't stay trapped in an unhappy marriage. Changes in the law.

> ☑ The first part of the answer identifies a reason (the spread of feminist views) and gives a brief explanation of how this is linked to the rise of the divorce rate

question

(2 + 2 marks awarded), but the second part simply identifies a factor (changes in the law) and gives no explanation, so cannot gain the additional 2 marks, giving 6 out of 8 marks in total. What could have been added to the second part as a suitable explanation?

(e) In most societies, divorce is on the increase, and Britain has one of the highest rates of divorce. The number of divorces has been going up since the 1970s when the law changed to make it easier. Nowadays people don't necessarily expect a marriage to be 'until death do us part', so the idea of divorce has almost become a part of marriage. About one in three marriages end in divorce.

There is some potentially relevant knowledge and understanding here, with information about rising divorce rates and a hint about changing attitudes to marriage. Is it strictly true to say that in 'most' societies divorce is on the increase? It largely depends on which part of the world and what kind of society you have in mind. While it is legitimate to start a question such as this with some 'background' information about divorce, this only becomes truly relevant if the information is picked up and carried through the rest of the answer. In this particular case, the discussion of the rise in the divorce rate has to be linked to the question of whether or not this is evidence of disenchantment with the institution of marriage.

One of the reasons for this is changes in women's attitudes. With the rise of feminism and women's lib, women have come to realise that they don't have to put up with an unhappy marriage if they don't want to. Also, if you have seen your parents get divorced, it will seem more normal to you. Divorce is also talked about a lot more, and lots of personalities and characters in the soaps are divorced or talking about getting divorced, so it is very much a part of society.

This paragraph gives some reasons why the divorce rate might have risen, but these are fairly simplistic and are not developed.

Feminists such as Barnard have shown that marriage is better for men than women, and a lot of married women become ill, so they must think 'Why should I put up with this?' This has led to a big increase in the number of lone-parent families, and the New Right believe that this is one of the causes of crime in society, while others say that it brings a lot of people into poverty.

A very brief mention of the feminist interpretation of health differences between married women and married men, but this is only weakly linked to the discussion. The discussion of lone-parent families, crime and poverty is not relevant to the question.

Still, quite a lot of people still do get married, and there is media interest in weddings, such as Posh and Becks. Also, some divorced people get married again (serial monogamy). It is hard to know for sure what is happening about marriage in society. There are a lot of couples who cohabit, and who therefore are as good as married, especially as in a lot of cases the law now treats them as though they were man and wife. Also, the age at marriage is rising, so a lot of people in their late twenties and thirties, who could be thought of as 'not going to get married', might marry when they are a bit older, when they have made a career or saved some money or done some of the things they want to, like travel the world.

📝 The answer here touches on 'marriage', the other part of the question. The comments about the number of marriages in society, media interest in 'weddings' and the remarriage of divorced people are all potentially relevant, though none is developed and allowed to further the discussion. However, some good points are made about the impact of cohabitation (should this be treated differently from 'marriage'?) and people who delay marriage rather than refrain from it.

So it is hard to say for sure that more divorce means that people are disenchanted with the institution of marriage.

📝 A very weak and ineffectual conclusion which does not arise logically from what has gone before.

📝 **Overall, the candidate shows a reasonable knowledge and understanding of the topic, though the relevance of some of the material to the question is not made explicit. There is some limited analysis and evaluation, for example about cohabitation and delayed marriage. The candidate scores 11 of the 20 available marks.**

Task Using the basic structure of this answer, rewrite it so that it would gain higher marks. The following points will help you.

- Take the first paragraph, and rewrite it, giving some information about divorce and marriage in Britain. Show how this information relates to the question, i.e. why is it significant in terms of what you are going to write later? Remember that the question is asking about the 'arguments' and the 'evidence' for the view in question.
- Take the second paragraph, and identify some brief reasons that have been suggested for the rise in divorce. You may wish to include feminist views here.
- Ignore the third paragraph of the answer, and write a new one, giving information about the rates of remarriage, and a brief discussion of ways in which the government and other bodies are trying to strengthen the institution of marriage. Is there any evidence you could produce that might support the idea of 'disenchantment' with marriage? For example, anything from surveys such as British Social Attitudes?
- Write a brief paragraph identifying some groups in society for whom the institution of marriage is still strong, and who may disfavour or even disallow divorce, such as particular religious or ethnic groups.
- Write a conclusion that sums up your arguments and clearly shows that you have answered the question.

(f) Item B says that feminist thought and practice have had a major influence upon the study of the family. Feminists such as Oakley have done studies on housework and shown that women are still responsible for most of the housework and childcare done in families, even though they are often breadwinners as well.

📝 The answer starts by including material from Item B, as instructed in the question, and gives an example of findings from feminist studies.

Item B also talks about domestic violence, which used to be 'swept under the carpet', but now, partly thanks to sociologists such as Dobash and Dobash, is more widely recognised as a major social problem.

📝 Another reference to Item B, this time picking up on the theme of domestic violence. Although Dobash and Dobash are mentioned, their contribution to the debate on domestic violence is not really made clear.

Feminists have also challenged the functionalist view that families are of benefit to society and everybody in them by pointing out how women in families can be exploited in a number of ways, such as how they are expected to be the carers of the sick and elderly and offer emotional support to the rest of the family.

📝 A contrast between functionalist and feminist views on the benefits of the family to individual members, thus introducing a theoretical point.

Feminists believe that we live in a patriarchal society, that is, a society where men have most of the power. This power is not only in society as a whole, but also in the family. In Victorian times, for example, women were really just like possessions, and had hardly any rights of their own. They were expected to obey their husband, and his word was law in the home. Although we have moved away from this situation, some of it is still there, in that in most families men are the major decision-makers and tend to have more authority than their wives. So feminist sociologists have shown that patriarchy still exists.

📝 The important concept of 'patriarchy' is introduced and explained, and a comparison made between Victorian and more modern times. The last sentence is expressed as a statement of fact, but no supporting evidence is given regarding *how* feminist sociologists have shown that 'patriarchy still exists'.

Willmott and Young believed that society was moving towards 'symmetrical families', where the roles of men and women in the family would be more equal. Feminists such as Oakley and Devine have shown that this is not really the case, and there is still a gendered division of labour within the family. Devine says that where men do some domestic work it is usually because they really have to, as their wives are out at work and they have to pitch in and give a hand.

📝 Some evaluative comments are made here, showing some feminist contributions to the debate on the symmetrical family.

So feminist sociologists have made an important contribution to the study of the family by showing that gender inequalities still exist.

An attempt is made to come to a conclusion regarding the contribution of feminist sociologists, but it is fairly simplistic, and seen only as showing that there are still gender inequalities.

Overall, this answer does not have a strong emphasis on the skills of analysis and evaluation, which are allocated 14 of the 20 available marks. There is reasonable knowledge and understanding of some feminist sociologists and their work, and some appropriate concepts are used. The main focus is on the domestic division of labour, and little is made of the broader theoretical perspective, namely the feminist challenge to 'malestream' sociology, and its contribution in taking aspects of 'family life' as topics worthy of sociological study. 'Feminist sociologists' are taken as a single group, and no attempt is made to distinguish between the views of, for example, radical and liberal feminists. The candidate scores 10 out of 20 marks.

Task Taking the basic structure of this answer, rewrite it so that it would gain higher marks. The following points will help you.

- Write an introductory paragraph that makes use of Item B, and that also tries, in more general terms, to summarise the importance of feminist sociologists to the study of the family, for example by emphasising its importance as an area of academic research, and/or by contrasting feminist views with those of some functionalist writers.
- Now write a series of brief paragraphs, each dealing with an aspect of family life to which feminist sociologists have made a contribution. These aspects could include domestic violence, housework and childcare, inequalities of power and decision-making, health, leisure time and pursuits, and the gendered socialisation of children. (There is no need to include all of these.) Make sure that you are able to show evaluation by drawing out the importance of the various contributions and, wherever possible, referring to a particular study rather than just making a general point.
- Write a paragraph showing that you recognise that there are different varieties of 'feminism' within sociology, and that feminist writers do not all agree on either the major source of gender inequality or how to overcome this.
- Write a brief conclusion that shows how, from what you have written earlier, feminist sociologists have made a contribution to the study of the family.

■ ■ ■

Answer to question 2: grade-A answer

(a) The number of marriages per thousand of the population that take place each year.

This accurately identifies the notion of a 'rate' (per thousand of the population) rather than just a 'number', and also indicates that the figure is almost always related to a particular year. The maximum 2 marks are awarded.

question

(b) The divorce rate has gone up, leaving many children with only one parent, usually the mother.

Having a baby outside of marriage is not such a stigma as it used to be, and a number of women are in this position.

Both these explanations are correct, for the maximum 4 marks. Can you think of any other explanations that could have been given?

(c) The woman may spend more time on housework and childcare than the man. The man may earn a lot more than the woman. The man may make the most important decisions in the family.

Three different areas of possible inequality are correctly identified — domestic division of labour, earnings and decision-making — so 6 out of 6 marks are awarded.

(d) In 1970, the law changed, making it much easier for couples to get divorced, and the divorce rate went up sharply, showing there were people who wanted a divorce, but had not been able to get one.

As divorce has become more common, and is not as shameful as it used to be, couples who are not getting on are much more likely to think of ending their relationship with a divorce. Many people will now have parents who are divorced, so it seems more normal to them.

Two correct reasons are identified, for 2 marks each. A suitable explanation is also given for each, for an additional 2 marks each, giving the candidate the maximum 8 marks.

(e) On the face of it, the rise in the divorce rate over the last 30 years or so seems to show that people do not believe in marriage as strongly as they used to. Even people who have got married in church and taken vows saying they will stay together 'until death do us part' now get divorced, sometimes after only a short period of marriage. After 1984, people could ask for a divorce after only 1 year of marriage. These changes in the divorce laws came about following major social changes in society, and a lot of pressure from people who did not believe that unhappy people should be made to stay married to each other.

A good introduction which shows an understanding of the title. The changes in the divorce laws are linked to changes in the wider society.

Before the Divorce Reform Act of 1969 (implemented in 1971), to get a divorce there had to be a 'guilty party', but after the Act this was changed, and the only reason needed for divorce was the 'irretrievable breakdown of marriage'. It has been estimated that if current trends continue, about two in five marriages will end in divorce.

A brief paragraph, showing further knowledge and understanding of the divorce laws. There is a danger that such information is not made relevant to the question, but here it is used to show knowledge of the extent of divorce in society.

However, this is not the whole picture. Although the divorce rate is high, about three in five marriages will not end in divorce, a fact that is often forgotten. Also, many divorced people will in fact remarry, showing that it is not marriage they are disenchanted with, but marriage to a particular person. More than two out of every five marriages are remarriages for one or both of the partners.

A useful paragraph, which shows that a simple look at the divorce rate does not give the whole picture. Analysis/evaluation skills are evident.

According to *Social Trends*, despite the growth in cohabitation, 'marriage is still the usual partnership between men and women'. Having said that, it is true that the actual number of marriages taking place is falling. There are now just over 300 000 marriages a year taking place, including remarriages, the lowest figure this century. However, the statistics suggest that the trend in rising divorces is levelling out, and that the rate is stabilising. There are a growing number of people who choose not to marry at all, the so-called 'singletons'. They may be disenchanted with the institution of marriage, though we would need research to tell us if this were true. If they are, it is obviously not linked to the divorce rate but is a separate phenomenon. It is also possible that some people, for example battered wives, are very disenchanted with marriage but they do not necessarily get divorced for a number of reasons, such as religion, finance or for the sake of the children.

A good paragraph which shows balance between the arguments and evidence being put forward and demonstrates all skill areas. It is always useful to show that you know and understand the different points of view and interpretations of the evidence.

Overall, we have had a period of rising divorces and falling marriages, which on the face of it would seem to suggest that the statement in the title is true. However, it could be argued that the fact that people divorce rather than remain in an unhappy marriage means that the institution of marriage is more, not less, important to them. We also have to take into account the high rate of remarriage; these people are obviously not disenchanted with marriage. A growing number of people are marrying more than twice, so we have a situation of serial monogamy. It has to be concluded, then, that a rise in the divorce rate does not necessarily mean that people are disenchanted with the institution of marriage.

This conclusion tries to draw together the main evidence and interprets it according to the requirements of the question. The final sentence shows clearly the conclusion reached by the candidate. It should be remembered that it is not always possible to do this; the arguments and evidence surrounding some topics are so complex that it is difficult to come to a firm conclusion. This is quite acceptable, provided that all the main points of view have been aired and the difficulty or impossibility of reaching a simple conclusion has been acknowledged.

> ✏ Overall this is a well-focused answer, showing good evidence of the skills. While a very brief mention was made of religious values, more could have been said about the impact of cultural norms and attitudes on people's views on marriage and divorce, showing how difficult it is to reach a simple conclusion on the link between divorce and ideas about marriage. The candidate scores 17 marks out of 20.

(f) The writer of Item B states clearly that feminist thought and practice have had a major influence on the study of the family. Before Ann Oakley's study of housework, 'malestream' sociology did not consider that issues such as housework, the division of labour within households and other gendered issues within families, such as power and decision-making, were topics worthy of serious sociological study. Feminist sociologists of all kinds, with their emphasis on the effects on both males and females of living in a patriarchal society, have brought issues of gender to the forefront, and such topics are now a normal part of sociology.

> ✏ A clear and concise introduction that refers to Item B and introduces the important concepts of malestream sociology, the gendered division of labour and patriarchal society.

The impact of feminist sociologists to the study of the family has been considerable, and aspects of family life that had been largely hidden from view have now been brought out, discussed and studied. Ansley, for example, has drawn attention to women's role as a 'sponge' to absorb their partner's (and sometimes their children's) frustration — what Ansley calls women's role as 'takers of shit'. Dobash and Dobash have done studies on the previously neglected area of domestic violence, and their findings have been supported by recent statistics showing that this is a large problem for society, and is actually becoming more widespread. Barrett and McIntosh have shown how there exists an 'ideology of familism', which spreads the message that family life is desirable for everyone, and the small independent nuclear family is the ideal. The Marxist feminists Abbott and Wallace have drawn attention to the role played by the family in maintaining patriarchy, the system that benefits men at the expense of women, and that also benefits capitalism. Feminists such as Oakley have also cast doubt on the view of the symmetrical family put forward by Willmott and Young, showing that the expected equality between men and women in the family has not taken place.

> ✏ A useful paragraph which brings in a number of different feminist sociologists and uses them to provide examples of the contribution made to sociological debates on the family. It is always useful, where possible, to provide actual examples to illustrate points, rather than just keeping the discussion at a general level.

As Item B says, differences in the experiences of men and women within the family are not just differences, they are actual inequalities, and these inequalities reflect inequalities in the wider society. Feminist sociologists have made an important contribution by making links in this way, showing that what happens in the family is not just an individual experience, but is linked to the structure, norms and values of society as a whole.

📝 Further reference is made to Item B, but this is not just quoted. The meaning is drawn out, showing an understanding of the material and how it relates to the question.

While some critics have argued that feminist perspectives on the family are flawed because they tend to treat all families as the same, and all women as suffering at the hands of men, there is no doubt that feminist sociologists have been of great benefit to the study of the family, bringing out issues that had not been studied before, and showing how both men and women are affected by a patriarchal system. Feminist perspectives have been useful in showing the other side to the functionalist view of family life as always beneficial to individuals and society as a whole. It is worth remembering that although we are now used to journalistic reports showing the rise in domestic violence, and the unequal division of labour in families between women and men, these issues were first raised by feminist sociologists, whose contribution to the study of the family has been considerable.

📝 A good evaluative conclusion which states a couple of criticisms of feminist views of the family, shows how feminist views have provided a counterbalance to functionalist views, and then summarises the arguments of the answer by concluding that feminist sociologists have made an important contribution to the study of the family. While there is a very brief reference to 'feminist sociologists of all kinds' and 'Marxist feminists', it would have been helpful to show awareness of other feminist perspectives.

📝 **Overall this is a sound, well-argued answer which sticks to the question and makes good use of relevant examples to support the arguments. Awareness is shown of Marxist and functionalist perspectives. The candidate scores 19 of the 20 marks available.**

uestion 3

Women in the labour market; changes in fertility; industrialisation and the family

Item A

The postwar years have been characterised by the growing participation of women in the labour market. This increase has come mainly from a considerable rise in the proportion of married women in paid employment, including those with dependent children. By 1999, 75% of married or cohabiting women of working age in the UK were employed or seeking work. However, many studies have shown that this rise of women in paid employment has not been accompanied by any significant changes in the gendered division of domestic labour.

Item B

Parsons's theory of the development of the family is set in a more general theory of social change. He argued that the preindustrial extended family was a multifunctional unit that met most of people's needs. Modernisation involved institutional differentiation, as specialised institutions emerged to meet particular needs. The family lost many of its functions to these other institutions.

Parsons argued that the nuclear form of the family was particularly well-suited to an industrial economy. Within this unit, roles were specialised, with one adult earning money through paid work and the other bringing up the children. There was a high rate of change in an industrial society, which required a mobile workforce prepared to move to where there was work. The small nuclear family, without obligations to an extended family and with only one 'breadwinner', could be geographically mobile. This close fit between the nuclear family and the requirements of the economy integrated the institutions of industrial society.

Source: adapted from Fulcher and Scott (1999) *Sociology*, Oxford University Press.

(a) **Explain what is meant by 'the gendered division of domestic labour' (Item A).** (2 marks)

(b) **Suggest *two* possible problems faced by mothers wishing to re-enter the labour market.** (4 marks)

(c) **Identify *three* reasons for the growing participation of women in the labour market in the last 50 years.** (6 marks)

(d) **Identify and briefly explain *two* criticisms of the functionalist view of the family.** (8 marks)

(e) **Examine the reasons for the fall in the fertility rate in Britain over the last 100 years.** (20 marks)

(f) Using material from Item B and elsewhere, assess the claim that industrialisation led to the break-up of the extended family.

(20 marks)

Total: 60 marks

■ ■ ■

Answer to question 3: grade-C answer

(a) Where women do the cooking and look after the children, and men do the DIY.

🖉 This is an *example* of the gendered division of labour rather than a definition of it. As such, it scores only 1 of the 2 marks.

(b) Their husband might think that they should stay at home and look after the child(ren), as this is what women should do. They might not know where to go to look for a job.

🖉 The first suggested problem just gets the 2 marks, although it might have been expressed in a more sociological manner. The second reason does not score any marks as it is not a problem specific to mothers wishing to re-enter the labour market — some people in other groups might experience the same difficulty.

(c) In a lot of jobs, women used to have to leave when they got married and now they don't, so women stay on or go back after they have children.

Girls just don't want to be housewives any more.

The family needs the money as the man doesn't earn enough or maybe is unemployed.

🖉 The first reason gains 2 marks, as it identifies a particular employment practice that used to remove many women from the labour market. The second (giving the student the benefit of the doubt) contains the germ of a sociological idea, namely changes in girls' expectations of their adult role, but it is expressed in a very simplistic and non-sociological manner — there is not sufficient detail there for the examiner to reward. The last point gains 2 marks, although again this is a case where a little more detail could have been provided, to make quite sure that the sociological point was clearly made. Overall, 4 of the 6 marks available are awarded.

(d) Functionalists say that families are good for individuals as well as society, but they don't take account of the fact that many people suffer in families, for example from domestic violence, child abuse. Their picture of the family is too rosy.

Functionalists say that only families can carry out the important functions of the family.

🖉 The first point gains 2 marks for identifying and 2 marks for briefly explaining a particular criticism. However, the second point is not at all clearly made (though you can probably work out what this student really meant to say) and does not score any marks. Rewrite this answer so that it would gain full marks.

(e) The fertility rate has fallen over the last 100 years, and there are many reasons for this, which I will now examine.

    This is not really a good way to start an answer. It more or less restates the question and does not help to set the scene for a sociological debate.

The fertility rate is the number of children born to women of childbearing age, and this has been falling, so that nowadays there are under two children in the average family, and some women don't have children at all. This means the population isn't being reproduced each generation, if you don't count immigration.

    It would have been a better idea to have started the answer with a definition of the fertility rate. This answer has not quite got it right — make sure you look up the correct definition of fertility rate if you are not sure, remembering that we are talking about a 'rate'. Knowledge is shown of the average number of children per family, and linked to the wider picture of the total population size.

In Victorian days, women tended to have large families. This is partly because contraception was not reliable and was not something talked about in society, and partly because large families were considered normal in society. Again, before the welfare state, people had to rely on their children to look after them in their old age, so they needed lots of children to do this.

    This demonstrates some reasonable knowledge and understanding of family size in the past, and gives reasons for the change to the smaller families of today. The point about what was considered 'normal' would have been worth developing, as family size is closely linked to social norms.

Nowadays children are taught about contraception and childbirth while they are at school, so there is no need for people to have children unless they want to. Although the functionalists believe that women should play the nurturing and expressive role in a family, a lot of girls now expect to have good jobs. Research has shown that they don't want to have to stay home 'chained to the kitchen sink' and looking after lots of children; they want to go out and do well in their career. This is due to the spread of feminist ideas, with women becoming much more career-minded. It also costs a lot of money to have children, so parents will think twice about it. A lot of babies used to die at birth or when they were very young (infant mortality rate), but things are a lot better now, with incubators and prema-ture baby units and vaccinations against childhood diseases.

    A number of points are made in this paragraph, all of them potentially relevant to the discussion, but their importance is not always drawn out and made clear. The first point is a little simplistic, or at least undeveloped, as despite greater knowledge and the availability of reliable contraception, many unplanned babies are still conceived, particularly in the case of teenage girls. The missing point is that if people really wish to limit their family size, the means are available for them to do so, but just the availability of reliable contraception does not automatically make

this happen. The next point, about women and employment, and the link to functionalist and feminist ideas, is an important one, and should have been developed
further. Rather than the phrase 'research has shown', it would have been much
better to mention one or two specific studies. The points about the cost of
bringing up children and the infant mortality rate are, of course, quite separate, and
certainly the point about the decline in the infant mortality rate is very important.
Note, however, that the reason why this is important to a discussion about the
decline in the fertility rate is not brought out — think about how this might have
been done.

One of the main reasons for the fall in the fertility rate is that women now have
a choice, and don't have to have babies unless they want to, whereas before they
didn't really have a choice, and just kept having baby after baby, even if it damaged
their health. When they got pregnant, there wasn't much they could do about it,
although there were some back-street abortionists, whereas nowadays even if an
accident happens you have got proper abortion clinics and abortion is legal. There
is also the 'morning after' pill if you think you might have got pregnant by mistake.

Again, the notion of women having a choice regarding pregnancy and childbirth is
important, and is worthy of further development. However, this choice is only
meaningful if women (and, of course, men) really do wish to limit their family size,
and this point should be linked back to some of the earlier discussion, where
possible reasons for this were mentioned.

While most families now have under two children, some families are much bigger.
A lot of working-class families and ethnic minority families have several children,
so the pattern isn't the same for all groups. Some groups have big families because
of their religion.

This is an evaluative point, showing that the pattern in fertility differs between
groups. Three factors are mentioned — social class, ethnicity and religion — and
each of these should have been expanded. It is not helpful to talk about 'ethnic
minority families' as though these were one homogeneous group. It is also worth
noting, of course, that social class, ethnicity and religion are not mutually exclusive
factors, but are interwoven. For example, the birth rate among working-class
Roman Catholics tends to be higher than among middle-class Roman Catholics, so
one attribute (social class) can partly override another factor (religion).

Sociologists recognise that human behaviour is influenced by many different
things, so it is probably true to say that there is no one single reason for the fall
in the fertility rate over the last 100 years. Different things have tended to work
together.

This is a good point, and helps to give the answer a slightly more sociological focus.

**Overall, the candidate has demonstrated some reasonable and relevant
knowledge and understanding of the issue, although the significance of many**

of the points remains implicit. A couple of evaluative points are made, though these are not developed. The candidate scores 12 marks out of 20.

(f) Item B says that the nuclear family was particularly well-suited to an industrial economy, and functionalists believe that industrialisation led to the break-up of the extended family. The nuclear family is smaller than the extended family and there is only one breadwinner, so the family can travel to where they are needed to work (geographically mobile).

> Relevant material is selected from Item B and the ideas are correctly identified as representing a functionalist view of the relationship between family structure and the economy.

If the functionalists are right, we should have extended families before indus-trialisation, and nuclear families after it, with a change-over period when there would be both types. Research done by Laslett and Anderson found that this wasn't true. Laslett used parish records to show that in preindustrial England there were not many extended families, and Anderson found from the Census of 1851 that a lot of workers in the textile industry were living in extended families. Willmott and Young found there were extended families in Bethnal Green in the 1950s, so the functionalists seem to have got it wrong.

> Use is made of the findings of Laslett, Anderson, and Willmott and Young to show that the functionalist view is not supported by empirical evidence. This demon-strates the skill of evaluation.

The situation today is that there are many kinds of family structure. We have nuclear families, extended families, lone-parent families, reconstituted families, empty-nest families and gay and lesbian families, as well as people living on their own, so there is not just one type.

> This is somewhat list-like in structure, but the point is put across regarding the diversity of family types in contemporary Britain. However, it is not shown how this point is linked to the discussion on the break-up of the extended family — you should always be sure to keep your information relevant to the discussion. How would *you* link this potentially important point to the question set?

It is not true to say that the extended family has broken up. Although a lot of people move about the country, some still live with or near to their extended family, for example some ethnic minority groups and people in rural areas. People can keep in touch by letter, etc. so they can be in contact even if they don't see each other very often. People also often turn to their family when they need help, such as borrowing money or looking after children or grandparents.

> Here are a few more points showing criticism of the view that the extended family has broken up, though these are not developed. Implicit in the evidence presented is the view that 'extended family' doesn't have to be defined as including co-residence, but this is not made clear, despite being an important aspect of the discussion.

The evidence shows, then, that the functionalists are wrong, and the extended family is still important to some people. They are also wrong because we have lots of different family structures, not just nuclear families.

🖉 This is a reasonably good attempt to sum up the preceding discussion, although the two points mentioned in the conclusion were not really brought out and sufficiently developed in the main body of the answer.

🖉 **Overall, the candidate has shown evidence of relevant knowledge and understanding of the topic, and also provided some criticism of the view under discussion, showing the skill of evaluation. However, the discussion throughout is rather 'thin', and the significance of many of the points to the set question is not brought out, so it is not easy to follow a clear line of argument. (10 marks out of 20)**

■ ■ ■

Answer to question 3: grade-A candidate

(a) This means when domestic tasks such as housework, childcare and DIY jobs are divided up and mainly performed by either the woman or the man. In most partnerships, women do most of the housework and childcare.

🖉 A brief but accurate explanation of the term for maximum marks. The additional sentence is added to make quite sure that the meaning is clear, although the marks would have been awarded without it.

(b) One problem would be that if their child or children were not of school age, they would need to find suitable and affordable childcare, which is not always easy, or find a job with a workplace crèche, which most workplaces do not have.

Another problem is that if the woman has been at home for a few years looking after children, she might be out of touch and find it difficult to get a job as she might lack the latest skills, for example working with computers.

🖉 Two possible problems are correctly identified for 4 marks, and expanded, although this was not asked for. If in doubt whether your meaning is made quite clear, it doesn't hurt to add an extra sentence, although always be mindful of how much time you have available.

(c) With the growth of feminist ideas, most women now accept that their main adult role should not only be as a housewife and mother, and they expect to return to work even if they have time off to have children.

Girls now leave school with as many, or even more, qualifications than boys. The country needs workers with suitable qualifications and employers can't afford to ignore half the potential workforce.

With the fall in the birth rate, women now spend far less time having and looking after children, and many women don't have children at all, so they are free to take paid employment.

🖉 Three acceptable reasons are given, for the maximum 6 marks. Other reasons that could have been offered are: that many families rely on a second wage to enable a desired standard of living; that many families are headed by lone mothers, who are the only breadwinner; and that much of the expansion in employment has been in the service sector and in what are traditionally regarded as 'women's jobs'. You will probably be able to think of additional reasons.

(d) The functionalist view suggests that families are beneficial for both individuals and for society as a whole, and tends to ignore the dysfunctional aspects of family life for some people, such as child abuse, domestic violence and the 'triple shift' undertaken by women.

Functionalists such as Parsons also believe that the best family type for modern society is the nuclear family, ignoring other types of family structure such as extended families, lone-parent families and even gay couples. The existence of these other types shows that society is capable of supporting a variety of family structures, and it is not possible to say that one type is 'better' than others.

🖉 Two criticisms are correctly identified (2+2 marks) and a suitable brief explanation of each provided (another 2+2 marks), giving the maximum 8 marks.

(e) The fertility rate refers to the number of live births each year per thousand women of childbearing age, and this has fallen steadily over the last century, although there have been peaks and troughs rather than a smooth decline. There are a number of factors that have an effect on the birth rate — economic, social, medical and even political.

🖉 A good start, with an accurate definition of the fertility rate, an outline summary of what has happened to it, and an identification of some important factors.

There was a sharp fall in the birth rate during the First and Second World Wars, when many young men were away fighting. However, in each case this was followed by a 'baby boom' when the birth rate rose sharply. In Russia, however, so many young men were killed that it took a generation for the birth rate to recover.

🖉 A brief paragraph, showing the effects of war on the birth rate, leading to both falls and increases, and a cross-cultural example making a contrast with Britain.

Economic factors are important; some of the lowest birth rates recorded in Britain occurred during the great depression of the 1930s, when many women resorted to illegal abortions to prevent having children they would not be able to feed and look after properly. Before the welfare state, people had children so that they could be looked after in their old age, but once benefits and old age pensions were brought in, this became unnecessary and contributed to families becoming smaller.

🖉 A different factor is identified and its effects explained. It is important that such information is not just left 'to speak for itself', but is expanded to show how it is relevant to the question.

Medical factors play a part. When the infant mortality rate was high, people had more children as they expected some of them to die in infancy from the terrible infectious diseases of the time. As these were slowly overcome, people realised that their children were increasingly likely to survive, and they did not have so many. Good and reliable contraception is important in reducing the number of babies born. However, people have to want to reduce their families (social norms and values), otherwise they will not take advantage of the available contraception, as some family planning programmes in the Third World are finding out. Feminists would argue that having fewer children reflects women's choice, including the choice not to have children at all.

🖉 A further factor is given a separate paragraph, which gives the answer a neat and logical structure. An evaluative point is made regarding the link between contraception and societal norms and values, with another cross-cultural example. A feminist viewpoint is also mentioned.

Although it seems rather strange, there is a link between the birth rate and the level of literacy in a society. As the literacy level rises, especially among women, the birth rate falls. This is probably because once women are literate, they are able to get better jobs, and do not wish to be restricted by having to look after a large family. Also, a society with increasing literacy is likely to be changing from an agricultural society to an industrial society, so more jobs needing literacy become available and open to women.

🖉 The effects of literacy are discussed with some evaluative points made. Use is also made of knowledge either from another subject, possibly geography or economics, or from the student's own general knowledge. Such links are always useful, and show how an answer does not have to be restricted only to information gained in sociology classes. However, it is important that such knowledge is made relevant to the question.

In today's society, most women want and expect to rejoin the labour force after having children, and wish to keep their child-rearing years to the minimum. They therefore have fewer children than their mothers and grandmothers. People also realise that it costs a huge amount of money to raise a child, and that they will be able to give their family a better standard of living with only one or two children rather than six or seven.

🖉 This paragraph could have been linked to the one discussing economic factors, but it is better to include relevant information, even if not in the ideal place, than to leave it out altogether.

Cultural factors are also important. Among many British people, it is now 'unfashionable' to have a large family, while among some ethnic minority groups, the reverse is true, making their families larger than the average. Religion also plays a part — Roman Catholic beliefs about contraception lead to Irish Catholics having some of the highest birth rates in the UK. Social class is another factor, although

the differences between the birth rates of the middle class and working class are not as big as they used to be. Working-class women still, on average, have more children than middle-class women. Age is another factor, linked to women's education and employment. As more and more women stay in education well beyond the official leaving age, and more women take up careers, the average age at first birth has risen, and is now in the late 20s. Obviously, if you don't start your family until you are nearly 30, you are likely to have fewer children than someone starting a family in their teens. New technologies can considerably extend the childbearing years, with women in their 50s and even 60s having children, though there are not many of these. This age pattern is also class-related, with working-class women tending to start their families earlier than middle-class women.

⯌ This paragraph mentions a range of factors, with suitable examples, and shows evaluation by indicating differences in the overall pattern.

There are therefore a number of reasons for the fall in the fertility rate, and it is not possible to say that any one is the most important, as many of them are linked and it is not really possible to separate them out.

⯌ A very brief but adequate conclusion, with an evaluative point regarding the problems of assessing the relative importance of the different factors discussed.

⯌ **Overall this is a well-focused and wide-ranging discussion, showing evidence of all skills and good use of examples. 18 out of 20 marks are awarded.**

(f) The functionalist view of family structure is that the dominant family structure in a society will be the one that best meets the particular 'needs' of that society at that time. As Item B states, in preindustrial society there was a need for families to be multifunctional, as few services were provided by the state and people's needs had to be met mainly by the family. This resulted, according to the functionalists, in most people living in three-generation, extended families.

⯌ Use is made of Item B, but the material is not just repeated, and it is made clear that the meaning is understood.

As Item B also states, Parsons believed that when society industrialised, there was a need for a different type of family structure, i.e. the nuclear family, with the adults playing specialised roles, one (the male) being the breadwinner, and the other (the female) being the homemaker and mother. This type of family also suited an industrial economy because it was geographically mobile, that is, the small family unit could easily travel and locate itself where the work was to be found.

⯌ There is further reference to Item B, although this is more like a repetition of the material and nothing is added. It is best to avoid this, as it is wasting valuable time.

This view has been criticised on the basis of empirical research. Firstly, the social historians Laslett and Anderson did separate studies on the preindustrial and newly industrial family structure. Laslett's findings were that in preindustrial England, only a small percentage of the population actually lived in three-generation, extended families, partly because of the low life-expectancy which meant that not many families managed to have three generations alive at the same time. Anderson looked at family structure in the newly industrialised towns of the north-west, and found that most people were actually living with kin in some form of extended family, which is not what the functionalists believed would be the case. The reason for this is that when people left the land and became wage labourers in the mills and factories, they needed their kinfolk who had moved out before them to help them find work and to provide them with accommodation and help in times of sickness. This shows that industrialisation, at least for a time, actually encouraged the growth of the extended family, not its break-up.

📝 Good use is made of the work of Laslett and Anderson, with their findings being explained, not just stated. An evaluative point is added at the end.

Another criticism arises from research that shows that the extended family in Britain did not die out, but is still important. It is true to say that not all extended families now live under the same roof, but if we take the frequency of contact, especially face-to-face contact, between members of a family as an indication of the existence of the extended family, then it is still very much alive. Willmott and Young's Bethnal Green research showed the matrifocal extended family alive and well in the 1950s, and Willmott's later study of North London in the 1980s also showed that different types of extended family were still very much in evidence. It is also true that in many ethnic minority communities, the extended family, even with people living under the same roof, is still a valued institution.

📝 This provides a further critical view of the functionalist standpoint, based on empirical research, and evaluation is demonstrated in recognising that there may be important differences in how the term 'extended family' is defined. It would have been helpful to have given an example from a particular ethnic minority group, for example Ballard on south-Asian families or Oakley on Cypriot families in Britain.

Willmott suggested that we should look not at the proximity (nearness) of relatives but at the contacts between them. He said that there were now three main types of kinship arrangement: the local extended family, the dispersed extended family and the attenuated extended family. More than half the people in his survey were in the first two types, that is, had regular and frequent contact with their wider family. Nowadays, with modern technology, it is much easier for people to keep in touch with relatives, even those who do not live close. More and more people have cars, special offers can mean even using public transport to visit can be quite cheap, most homes are on the telephone, and a growing proportion of people have e-mail. It is true that family structures have altered, and there are more lone-parent families and more people living alone. However, it is not possible to say that these changes were caused by industrialisation, and the research shows that most people do, in fact, keep in contact with at least some family members, and turn to them when they need help.

🖉 This shows good and relevant knowledge of Willmott's later research, with some evaluative comments at the end.

It is not possible to say, therefore, that industrialisation led to the break-up of the extended family, although how we define extended family may have changed, as we do not expect people living under the same roof to be considered an extended family.

🖉 This is a brief conclusion, but one that sums up the main argument presented in the answer.

🖉 **Overall, the candidate has made excellent use of relevant knowledge, and produced an answer that remains focused on the question. An evaluative tone is present throughout, good use is made of sociological concepts and there is a logical structure to the answer. The candidate is awarded 19 out of 20 marks.**

The symmetrical family; family structure; the role of the extended family

Item A

Young and Willmott introduced the concept of 'symmetry' in 1973 as part of their 'march of progress' theory of the family. Although they maintained that women still took the major responsibility for domestic labour and childcare, they believed that men were spending an equivalent amount of time on home-related activities. The couples had become home-centred; they spent most of their leisure time together and their conjugal relationship was companionate. However, this work has been criticised from many different standpoints.

Current research on conjugal roles and the division of domestic labour has moved away from a quantitative examination of time spent over domestic tasks to an exploration of the perceptions of couples with regard to the fairness of their division of household labour. This newer work has shown that couples do not approach domestic tasks like time and motion efficiency managers, but are engaged in complicated personal and social agendas about masculinity, femininity, intimacy and care.

Source: adapted from Marsha Jones (1997) 'The symmetrical family revisited', *Sociology Review*, Vol. 6, No. 3.

Item B

Today, a new stereotype of kinship holds sway: a view that, however it may have been in the past, the research of the 1950s and 1960s was describing a high point of urban kinship that was near the end of its reign. Since then, it is held, a number of changes have broken the old order: high levels of geographical mobility, redevelopment of the inner areas of Britain's cities and industrial towns, changes in the family and marriage, and the increase in the number of wives going out to work.

But that is not the end of the story. If one looks not at the proximity of relatives but at contacts between them, a different picture comes into focus. A number of recent surveys have shown that between about two-thirds and three-quarters of people of all ages still see at least one relative at least once a week. Evidence from recent studies shows that relatives continue to be the main source of informal support and care.

Source: adapted from Peter Willmott (1988) 'Urban kinship past and present', *Social Studies Review*, Vol. 4, No. 2.

(a) **Explain what is meant by 'conjugal roles' (Item A).** (2 marks)

(b) **Identify** *two* **criticisms that have been made of the ideas of Willmott and Young on the 'symmetrical family'.** (4 marks)

(c) **Suggest** *three* **ways in which women's domestic roles have changed over the last 50 years.** (6 marks)

(d) **Identify and briefly explain** *two* **reasons why 'a quantitative examination of time spent over domestic tasks' might not give an accurate picture of conjugal roles and the domestic division of labour.** (8 marks)

(e) **Identify and explain some of the changes that have taken place in family structure over the last 50 years.** (20 marks)

(f) **Using material from Item B and elsewhere, assess the view that the extended family no longer plays a significant role in family life in modern Britain.** (20 marks)

Total: 60 marks

■ ■ ■

Answer to question 4: grade-A candidate

(a) Conjugal roles refer to the roles in the family played by husbands and wives, or by partners if the couple are not married. Usually it means how couples divide up domestic tasks and childcare, and also whether they spend their leisure time together or apart. Bott identified joint and segregated conjugal roles.

> A rather long answer, but one that makes the understanding of the concept quite clear, for maximum marks. If just the first sentence had been offered, there might have been some doubt in the examiner's mind whether the student really had a good understanding of the concept, but the second sentence removes any doubt. The third sentence emphasises the student's knowledge of the concept, but the answer would have got the marks without it.

(b) Feminists argue that roles have not become more symmetrical and that women still do much more than men in the home, even when the women are in paid employment.

Other sociologists argue that Willmott and Young did not take account of family diversity, and that there are many different ways of organising family life, i.e. they seemed to assume that all families would be more or less the same.

> Two appropriate criticisms of the views of Willmott and Young, for full marks. Other criticisms that could have been offered include questioning the idea of the 'march of progress' of the family, ignoring negative aspects of family life; questioning whether it is the case that the working class will follow the example of the middle class in family roles and structures (the principle of 'stratified diffusion'); and the Marxist-feminist argument that the concept ignores the power differences between men and women in a patriarchal society.

(c) Three ways in which women's domestic roles have changed are:

- women spend a smaller part of their lives looking after children as families have become much smaller
- women now have lots of labour-saving devices to make housework easier, such as washing machines and dishwashers
- women are now usually a breadwinner as well as housewife/mother

Three acceptable changes are offered, for full marks. Alternatives could have included: the greater involvement of male partners in some domestic tasks; the increased proportion of women who are lone parents and therefore the sole adult in the family; and the growth in the number of women who remain single and childless.

(d) It might not give the whole picture. If the sociologist just asks people how much time is spent on different things, and who does what in the house, it might seem unfair, but it could be that the couple have talked it over and actually chosen to do it that way. Some women really enjoy gardening, for example, and want to do most of it, and in some families it's the man who does most of the cooking. Also the woman might only work part-time and therefore have more time at home than her partner.

People might not be telling the truth. Research has shown that men over-estimate the time they spend on domestic tasks and women under-estimate the time, as often the women are doing lots of different things at once.

Two reasons are given (2 + 2 marks), and each is explained (2 + 2 marks). Sometimes it is possible, as here, to give a reason in a brief sentence, and then write a sentence or two as an explanation, while at other times the identification and the explanation are woven together. In either case, it is important to remember to explain clearly what you have identified.

(e) It is probably true to say that there has always been considerable diversity in family structure in Britain. In the past, some families were extended families while others were unable to reach this state because of the early death of the adults. Many families were also headed by a lone parent due to the death of one of the parents, either the mother, often in childbirth, or the father, perhaps killed in a war or an accident at work.

This is a good introduction which not only focuses on the main aspect of the question, but raises an important point that is often overlooked, namely that diversity in family structure is not a new phenomenon.

However, over the past 50 years, several changes in family structure have occurred because of a variety of changes in society. Society as a whole has become much more tolerant and accepting of different family structures, although government policies still seem to promote a particular kind of family, notably the small, nuclear family.

The focus now moves to the timescale stated in the question, namely the last 50

years, and links changes in family structure to changes in society — an important point. The last phrase, about government policies, is not developed but makes an important evaluative point.

One of the changes that has affected family structure is the fall in the birth rate. Most couples now have just one or two children and a growing number don't have any. The decrease in the number of children means that the proportion of families with dependent children, especially nuclear families with two parents, has fallen. At the other end of the scale, increased life-expectancy means that there are many more three- and four-generation families, even though they probably won't live under the same roof. There has also been a rise in so-called 'empty-nest' families, where the couple's children have grown up and left home.

e Points here are not just made and left to 'speak for themselves', but are explained and related to the focus of the question. The concept of 'empty-nest' families is introduced and explained briefly.

Changes in the divorce laws have resulted in a significant proportion of marriages ending in divorce, and this has led to an increase in the number of families headed by a lone parent. Another result of divorce has been the rise in the number of step-families, as serial monogamy has led to many people marrying for a second or even a third time. Another reason for the rise in lone-parent families is the changing attitude towards children born out of wedlock. It used to be seen as a terrible thing for an unmarried woman to have a baby, and some women were shut away by their families, or abandoned by them, or forced to give the baby up for adoption. This has changed, and now over a third of all births take place outside of marriage. Many of these babies, however, are born to couples in a stable relationship, as marriage has declined in popularity, and a considerable number of couples now cohabit, which used to be frowned upon and called 'living in sin'.

e Good points are made about divorce and one of its consequences for family structure. Other reasons for the rise in lone-parent families are also offered.

Another change in society has been the growing number of immigrants from different parts of the world. These ethnic minority groups bring their traditional family structures with them from their home society. So there are some groups with a tradition of large families, some with a very strong extended family structure, some with a tradition of matriarchy and others with joint families, that is, two or more brothers and their wives and children living as a family.

e This introduces another factor influencing changes in family structure, and shows recognition that there are differences between different ethnic minority groups, though the groups referred to could have been mentioned by name.

Although not everyone would agree to call gay and lesbian couples 'families', there has been an increase in the number of same-sex couples, and a growing number of these have children. Some lesbian couples contain the natural child of one of the women, and recently a lesbian couple was allowed to adopt a child. There has even been a case where two gay men had children — a surrogate mother gave birth to twins with one of the men as the natural father. Though such cases are not that common, it is an example of another type of family structure. Again, a growing number of people live alone, including the elderly widowed, divorced people without children, and a number of 'singletons' — young unmarrieds who choose this way of life.

🖉 This broadens the discussion to include less common types of family structure. Strictly speaking, people living alone are a 'household' rather than a 'family', but positive marking means that there are no 'penalties', and, in any case, it could be argued that the point being made has some relevance.

Functionalists would say that the family structures we have reflect the needs of the whole society, while Marxists would argue that we have the structures that are best for a capitalist economy. Feminists still believe that all aspects of society, including family structure, are influenced by patriarchy. The postmodern view is that people will choose the type of family structure they think is the best for them.

🖉 Perhaps a belated recognition that there are some theoretical points to be made, but these are tied into the question.

There have been many important changes in society over the last 50 years, many of them relating to changes in the rights and roles of women. Their impact can be seen on family structure, leading to such a wide range of family types that it is not possible to say that any one is 'normal'.

🖉 A brief conclusion relating back to the title, and making an important final point about 'normality' in family structure.

🖉 **Overall, the candidate has provided a wide-ranging and well-focused answer, with good evidence of all the skills, and scores 18 marks out of 20. The answer has a logical structure leading to a brief but relevant conclusion.**

(f) As Willmott says in Item B, there is a new stereotype of kinship, where social changes have led to the extended family becoming much less important than it was in the past, such as in the 1950s and 1960s, when Willmott and Young did their research into family life in Bethnal Green. If this is true, it would support the functionalist view that the nuclear family is the most suitable family type for an industrial society.

🖉 A good introduction which makes immediate reference to Item B, identifies the part that links to the question, shows knowledge of the Bethnal Green research and makes an evaluative point regarding the link to the functionalist view.

The Bethnal Green research showed a working-class community where there was not much geographical mobility, with most people living in the same small area in which they had grown up, and where there was frequent day-to-day contact

between family members, especially daughters and their mothers. The families were highly 'mum-centred' (matrifocal), and few of the women went out to work, leaving them time to visit and go shopping with their mothers and sisters.

> This demonstrates further relevant knowledge of the kind of extended family relationship found by Willmott and Young, though it would have been unwise to write much more on this, as the focus of the question is on the situation now.

It is true that there have been many important social changes that have had an effect on the frequency of face-to-face contact between people and their wider kin. One of these is geographical mobility. When Willmott and Young studied families who had moved from Bethnal Green to the suburb of Greenleigh, which was only 30 miles away, they found that the families had become more home-centred and privatised, and that the wives didn't have such regular contact with their mothers, and had developed a more companionate relationship with their husbands.

> This picks up on one of the factors mentioned in Item B, and applies it to later research by Willmott and Young. Good use is made of appropriate sociological concepts.

However, how the evidence is interpreted depends on what definition of 'extended family' is being used. If it means regular, daily, face-to-face contact, then it is probably true to say that the extended family has declined in importance. Should we use this definition, though? Fiona Devine went back in the early 1990s and looked at car workers and their families in Luton, revisiting a study first carried out by Goldthorpe and Lockwood. Devine argued that the amount of privatisation in the family had been exaggerated, as her findings showed that most couples did keep in regular contact with their kin; not only their parents, but also their siblings. Such contact has been made easier with the spread of car ownership and telephones. Finch and Mason (1993), in their study of families in Manchester, also found that people still relied heavily on kin for a range of help and advice, things such as financial help, emotional support and looking after children. As Item B shows, Willmott's own later research, using the number of contacts between relatives rather than just face-to-face meetings, showed that most people keep up contacts, with a high proportion still seeing at least one relative at least once a week. Willmott says that there is only a very small proportion of people who have virtually no contact at all with their relatives. He identifies three forms of the modern extended family, which he calls the local extended family (relatives who live close to each other and see each other regularly), the dispersed extended family (face-to-face contact is less because they don't live nearby, but there is frequent contact), and the attenuated extended family (where contact is much less frequent). Willmott said that about half the adult population were in a dispersed extended family. The growing use of e-mails and the Internet, especially among older people, means that it is even easier for people to keep in touch with relatives, even when they live thousands of miles away.

> ✏ This paragraph has an evaluative tone throughout, and uses appropriate research to illustrate the point that the extended family is still relevant, although the definition of the term has been modified. It makes good use of studies and demonstrates sound knowledge of appropriate concepts.

It is also true that a number of families, especially the women in them, look after elderly relatives in some way. The policy of 'care in the community' has meant an increase in the number of elderly people who have to be looked after outside of care institutions, and for many of them it has meant care in, or by, the family. Such responsibilities are some of the factors that lead many women to work part-time rather than full-time.

> ✏ This provides further evidence that challenges the view expressed in the question.

Among some Asian ethnic minority groups, the extended family plays a very important role, and such families are very likely to have three-generation families living under one roof, or at least to have regular face-to-face contact.

> ✏ This recognises different cultural norms and practices among different groups in society.

Another problem facing sociologists is that many of the views about the so-called 'golden age of the family' are actually myths and not based on hard evidence. It is very difficult to prove that close contacts with relatives and giving and receiving help among relatives was actually that much greater in the past than it is today.

> ✏ A further important and evaluative point.

The view that the extended family no longer plays a significant role in family life in modern Britain does not seem to be supported by sociological evidence. Relatives are still a major source of help for most people, and contact is maintained even though this might not be frequent face-to-face contact. What has happened is that our definition of 'extended family' has become modified.

> ✏ A brief conclusion which relates to the question and summarises the main points made throughout the answer.

> ✏ This is a very good answer which stays focused on the question, shows good skills, especially evaluation, and a range of appropriate knowledge. The candidate scores the maximum 20 marks.

Representations of the family; family roles; the functions of the family

Item A

A social historian with a special interest in family matters, John Gillis, has usefully made a distinction between 'the families we live with' and 'the families we live by'. The 'families we live with' are the families we experience every day, with all their messiness, their pains and their joys. Here people may be competitive, uncaring or oppressive; but they may also be supportive, warm or understanding.

The 'families we live by' are more to do with the images and representations of the family that confront us in numerous ways. These appear as myths about families of the past and the present and the ways in which these myths frequently become part of the many family rituals that are often followed and enjoyed.

A historical perspective, such as the one provided by Gillis, may provide a useful corrective to stories about 'the golden age' in the past, when families were more stable, more unified and more caring. These myths may not only continue to influence our view of the past but also continue to influence our present as we attempt to reconstruct them through rituals such as Christmas celebrations or weddings.

Source: adapted from David Morgan (1998) 'Thinking about family life', *Sociology Review*, Vol. 7, No. 4.

Item B

The functionalist view of the family has emphasised the important functions performed by families for both individuals and society as a whole. Among these important functions are the primary socialisation of children, the preparation of the young to fulfil adult worker roles in society, the socially approved satisfaction of sexual needs, the contribution of the family as an economic unit and what Parsons called the 'stabilisation of adult personalities'. By this he meant that the family provided the emotional warmth and security to enable its members to cope with the stresses and strains of the wider society.

Functionalist views of the family have been criticised by sociologists from a range of perspectives. One argument is that the family in modern societies has progressively been stripped of many of its so-called essential functions, as these have increasingly been taken over by other, specialist, agencies.

(a) **Explain what is meant by 'representations of the family' (Item A).** (2 marks)
(b) **Give examples of *four* 'family rituals' other than those mentioned in Item A.** (4 marks)

(c) Identify *three* ways in which social historians have shown that family life in the past should not be thought of as a 'golden age'. (6 marks)

(d) Identify and briefly explain *two* ways in which the realities of family life for many people differ from the 'romanticised' view often portrayed by the media. (8 marks)

(e) Outline the arguments and evidence for the view that the roles of both men and women in the family have changed significantly over the last 50 years. (20 marks)

(f) Using material from Item B and elsewhere, assess the view that the family in modern society has been stripped of so many of its functions that it can no longer be seen as a significant social institution. (20 marks)

Total: 60 marks

■ ■ ■

Answer to question 5: grade-C candidate

(a) How the family is shown in the media — not necessarily a true picture.

🖉 Essentially a correct answer, although rather brief, and possibly an example would have ensured that the meaning was absolutely clear. However, this is sufficient to gain the 2 marks.

(b) Funerals; children's birthday parties; engagement parties; Easter.

🖉 The first three each qualify for a mark, but the last one, 'Easter', does not suggest a family ritual, and would need an explanation to gain a mark.

(c) Most people were very poor and had hardly enough to eat. The death rate was high so there were a lot of widows and orphans. People were often very unhappy.

🖉 The first two answers, dealing with poverty, hunger and the consequences of a high death rate, are acceptable for 2 marks each, but the third one is just too vague to qualify for the marks. Can you think of a suitable answer to replace it?

(d) Advertisers show families as being happy, smiling and healthy, whereas many people live in families where there is a lot of stress and illness.
A lot of people live on their own and not in a family.

🖉 These answers are rather brief for this type of question. The first one just about manages to get the 2+2 marks, but the second really only 'identifies' a way and does not go on to explain it, and so gets only 2 marks.

(e) Roles in the family have changed a lot in the last 50 years. More couples cohabit, and the divorce rate has risen tremendously as well. There are a lot of lone-parent families and also many 'singletons' who don't want to get married at all.

🖉 Apart from the simplistic statement in the first sentence, this paragraph is more about changes in family structure than family roles. Although the two are linked (for example, lone-parent families are by definition headed by a lone parent, which is a role), it is important to show that you understand the difference, and to be sure to focus on what the question has asked.

With the rise of feminism, women have become more independent and are usually breadwinners alongside the men, even if they have children. Even so, they still do most of the housework and look after the children more than the men do, so one part of the role hasn't changed much.

℮ Two good points are made here, one showing a change in women's role, the other an evaluative point stating that one aspect of women's traditional role hasn't changed completely. It would have been better had the latter point, at least, been supported by some sociological evidence.

Women nowadays don't have as many children as they used to, and quite a lot of women don't have any. There are lots of labour-saving devices such as washing machines, freezers and microwaves, so women don't have to spend as much time on housework. The rise of the New Man means that men do more in the home than they used to, though feminists don't really believe that the New Man exists.

℮ These are potentially relevant points, but it is not made explicit how they link to the question and further the argument being made. No supporting evidence is offered for the points made about the New Man.

Girls always used to think that when they left school they would soon marry, have a family and be a housewife, but girls don't think that any more. The housewife role is not seen as the be all and end all for a woman, and nowadays girls expect to go out to work and have a career, even if they get married and have children. Women in today's society play more roles than they did 50 years ago and there are more opportunities for them. They have equal rights to men even if this doesn't always work out in practice, for example they still get paid less than men.

℮ An important point about changes in women's perception of their role in society is being made here, but again its relevance to the argument is not clearly drawn out. This is a case where it would have been good to refer to an actual research study. An evaluative point is made regarding the alleged equality between men and women.

So, overall, women's role in society has changed a lot over the last 50 years, although in some aspects the change hasn't been as big as you might have expected.

℮ This is a weak conclusion which adds little to what has already been written.

℮ **Overall, the candidate has made some good points, although often their relevance to the question is not made explicit. The candidate has failed to deal with the part of the question that asks about changes in the role of men, emphasising how important it is to read the question carefully and make sure that you do all that you are asked. Virtually no 'evidence' is offered in support of the points being made, and there is little reference to the 'arguments' put forward about changing roles. The candidate scores 10 marks out of 20.**

Task Write an answer to this question that would achieve higher marks. Try to include the following points.

- What 'arguments' are put forward to suggest or explain changes in the roles of men and women in the family over the past 50 years?
- What aspects of conjugal roles might be considered? Obvious ones are concerned with housework and childcare, but you could also consider power, decision-making, leisure pursuits and the expectations of men and women in a partnership.
- What sociological evidence could you use to support your points?
- How would you decide on the significance of the changes you discuss?
- Would it be true to say that the changes apply to all men and women? If not, why?

(f) As Item B says, functionalists believe that the family performs important functions for individuals and for society as a whole. These include primary socialisation, education, sexual gratification, the economic function and the stabilisation of adult personalities. This view has been criticised by many sociologists, and some people believe that the family has now been stripped of most of its functions.

🖉 This paragraph does little more than repeat, albeit in slightly different words, what has been said in Item B. 'Using' material does not mean simply copying it.

But is this true? A lot of people would argue that the family is still important in society. After all, most of us still live in families, and families provide for their members in a lot of different ways. Take the economic function. In the olden days, people worked together as a family, growing or making things for their own use and to sell, so they were an economic unit. Even children had to work, in the fields or at home helping to spin and weave. Nowadays families don't live like this, although there are some family businesses, like when members of an extended Asian family all work in the family shop. However, the family has moved from being a unit of production to a unit of consumption. This means that families 'consume' (buy) things as a unit. Houses, cars, washing machines, food and even holidays are usually bought by families rather than by individuals. The government also gives money to families, such as the child allowance.

🖉 This shows some knowledge and understanding of the economic function of the family past and present, and uses a general evaluative tone in that the implicit point being made is that the family still has an economic function to perform.

Even though children have to go to school from ages 5–16, a lot of teaching (education) still goes on in the family. Children already have a lot of knowledge before they go to school, and many children still learn things in the family even though they go to school, such as when their parents buy them computers or books or take them to museums.

🖉 Another evaluative point about the educational function of the family today.

Also, most families do still help their members in lots of ways. Women in particular play the role of 'takers of shit' within the family, and most people will talk out their problems in the family, at least until they leave school.

🖉 A brief point. The relevance is not really brought out.

The government thinks that the family is still important, and is always talking about the importance of the family and bringing in policies to support the family. On the other hand, you could argue that the high rates of teenage pregnancies and the divorce rate show that, for many people, the family is not as important as it used to be.

🖉 The first point could be developed, and examples given of policies designed to support the family. The second sentence is rather simplistic, and it is not explained why teenage pregnancies and a high divorce rate should indicate that the family is not as important as it used to be, at least for some people. Points like this should not be left to 'speak for themselves', but their relevance to the argument should be explained.

Although the functions of the family have changed over time, it is not possible to say that it is no longer a significant social institution, as it still has many important functions that are not carried out by anything else in society.

🖉 This is a weak attempt at a conclusion. The 'many important functions' should be stated briefly and should, of course, be those discussed in the preceding paragraphs.

🖉 **There is an evaluative thread running through this answer which, at least implicitly, argues that some of the functions of the family, although changed, are still carried out and are still (presumably) important. However, little reference is made to the argument that other, specialist, agencies have taken over many of the family's functions. There is little evidence in this answer that the student has made a sociological study of the family — no reference to studies and no sociological theories or perspectives other than functionalism. The candidate scores 8 out of 20 marks for this question.**

Task Rewrite this answer after you have made relevant notes from your textbooks on this issue. Make sure that you include appropriate sociological concepts and evidence, and refer to other sociological theories and perspectives.

■ ■ ■

Answer to question 5: grade-A candidate

(a) Ways of showing family roles, structures and situations in a particular way, such as in television and cereal advertisements, TV sitcoms and soaps, newspaper stories, etc.

🖉 Full marks are awarded for a suitable definition. This is one of those questions in which it is often easier to illustrate, and therefore make the meaning of the concept clear, by using examples. However, giving examples alone, without attempting a definition, will lose marks.

(b) Christenings; Diwali; funerals; bar mitzvahs

📝 Four appropriate examples, for full marks. Had Christmas celebrations or weddings been offered as an answer, neither would have scored a mark, as both these were mentioned in Item A. The answer also shows recognition of Britain as a multi-cultural society.

(c) Infant mortality was high, so a large proportion of families had to cope with the death of a child.

Poor children received no schooling and were sent out to work in mines and factories, etc. from a very young age.

Women had virtually no rights, for example they could not own property or vote, and were thought of almost as the property of their husbands.

📝 Three relevant examples are given, for full marks. Among other factors that could have been mentioned are: the widespread existence of domestic violence, poverty and disease; the lack of notions of 'romantic love' (among the wealthy, many marriages were virtually arranged); the lack of any state provision for the sick and elderly; and the virtual impossibility of obtaining a divorce.

(d) Most soaps and sitcoms show families living in large, comfortable, well-furnished houses, where children have their own rooms, while in reality many families live in poor, overcrowded accommodation or even in bed-and-breakfasts. Many families on the breadline couldn't even begin to afford most of the things that are shown in the adverts.

Lots of stories in magazines like *Hello* show families with famous parents who can carry on with their careers because they have full-time nannies and domestic help, while most working women have to bear the 'triple shift' of paid work, responsibility for running the home and looking after the children, and also giving emotional support to the family.

📝 Two appropriate reasons are identified (good accommodation and relative wealth; help with, or even freedom from, domestic work and childcare), and each of these is satisfactorily explained, for maximum marks.

(e) Fifty years ago, most married women (and there were not many women who would have been cohabiting) would have been full-time housewives, especially if they had children. They spent long hours on housework (77 hours a week — Oakley). In some jobs, women actually had to leave work as soon as they got married. In the programme *Out of the Doll's House*, we saw that some women had no idea what their husband earned each week, and they were just given some money to pay for the food, etc. and had no money at all of their own. The man was expected to be the breadwinner, and to look after all the financial affairs of the family. He was also expected to be the one who knew about politics and 'outside' affairs, and his opinions were the ones that mattered. Most men expected a clean home and the dinner on the table when they got home from work. Looking after the children was the woman's job, although the father was the one in charge of discipline if the children were naughty ('Wait till your father gets home!'). Couples expected to have to live together for life, and divorce was frowned upon.

📝 A very full paragraph, which might have benefited from being split up, and one that gives a number of examples of 'typical' male and female roles within the family. It demonstrates good knowledge and understanding of a range of features and makes references to Oakley's study and a television documentary.

Women were traditionally close to their mothers, as shown in Willmott and Young's 'Family and kinship in East London', and many women lived close to their family of origin. Families were larger than today, as birth control was still unreliable (no pill until the 1960s), and abortion was frowned upon. Some women put their lives at risk by having 'back-street abortions' if they got pregnant. Most women were thought of as being not as intelligent as men.

📝 Further knowledge and understanding of aspects of the female role are evident here, with reference made to a sociological source.

Nowadays, many of these things have changed. Most women are breadwinners in their own right, and contribute to the family earnings, while many women are the sole earner in their family, either as a lone parent or because their husband is unemployed. Women have a choice as to whether or not to get married, and a large proportion of couples cohabit. Marriages have become more 'companionate', and many couples don't live near either set of parents. Women can now take charge of their own fertility, and families have got smaller. With the rise of the 'New Man', couples are more likely to share at least some domestic tasks and childcare, and women have a more equal say in family affairs. Both men and women know that they don't have to stay trapped in an unhappy marriage; they can apply for a divorce, which is quite easy to get.

📝 This provides the contrast between 'now' and '50 years ago'. It might have been better to divide the discussion more equally between the two periods, although most of the points raised regarding the earlier period are revisited here.

On the other hand, there are some ways in which the roles haven't changed as much as we might think. Women still do the bulk of housework and looking after children, even though they go out to work, and society still regards men as the dominant partners. Men still feel that they have a responsibility to provide a good standard of living for their family. There is still domestic violence, usually against women, despite women having more rights.

📝 Evaluation is shown here by a critical look at the extent of the changes — 'not as much as we might think'. Some supporting evidence of this is provided.

There have been some important changes, but there are still differences within families based on class and ethnicity.

📝 This is potentially a very important point, and it is a pity that this was not developed, at least to the extent of briefly outlining what some of the class and ethnic differences might be. In order to do this, some of the earlier material would probably have to be cut.

ⓔ **Overall the candidate has shown good knowledge and understanding, supported by some relevant examples and reference to studies. The point about class and ethnic differences could have done with a little more development, but there was evidence of analysis and evaluation. The candidate scores 15 marks out of 20.**

(f) The argument expressed in Item B is that in modern societies the family is less important than it was, as many of its functions have been taken over by specialist agencies. Among these would be: the education function, taken over by formal schooling; the health function, taken over by the NHS; looking after the elderly and unemployed, taken over by the pensions and benefits systems; and the economic function, with the family no longer an economic work unit. With the development of in vitro fertilisation and other fertility treatments, it could also be argued that even the reproduction of children is no longer exclusively a family function.

ⓔ This shows a clear understanding of the view expressed in Item B, supported by relevant knowledge of the main aspects of the argument.

According to this view, the family has been so stripped down that it has very few functions left, and these are presumably thought to be not very important.

ⓔ This acts as a brief summary of the view, prior to presenting the main points of the argument.

However, is this really the case? Marxists would not agree, as in their view the family still serves the needs of capitalism by raising the next generation of workers, providing a reserve army of labour of women and unemployed men, and by giving workers a haven from the stresses and strains of the exploited proletarian workforce. Marxists would also argue that because the family still provides workers with food and shelter and clean clothing, wages can be kept low, as these things are cheaper in the family than if they had to be paid for from wages.

ⓔ This provides evidence against the view (evaluation) drawn from the Marxist perspective, and again shows good knowledge and understanding of the relevant points.

Feminists would also not agree with the view in Item B. Even though most of them see the family as a source of oppression for women, they would not deny its importance. In fact, some see it as important just because it is one of the main sources of oppression for women. The family is one of the sources of patriarchy, and helps to maintain a patriarchal society.

ⓔ Further views against the argument (more evaluation), this time drawn from the feminist perspective.

What of the idea that many family functions have now been taken over? If we look at education, while it is true that children are educated in schools, they also receive a lot of education at home, especially the important things like learning to talk and other aspects of primary socialisation, without which they would be more difficult to educate. Parents and families still provide books, computers and other aids to education, and families support schools in lots of ways, for example fund raising. Most families are also involved in helping their children to find suitable jobs, and for children who go on to university, families play a large part in giving them financial support. If they didn't, many students couldn't go into higher education at all. Even with healthcare, people are still looked after by their families when they are ill. Families care for people with minor illnesses, while with major ones, families have to look after people when they come home from hospital.

This paragraph offers some empirical evidence against the view that the family has been stripped of many of its functions, and shows evaluation as well as good knowledge and understanding.

With regard to finance, even with pensions and unemployment benefit and other state help, research shows that most people still look to their family for different kinds of help and support. Families (women) still look after the elderly, grandparents often help with childcare, financial help may be given to young couples by their parents, etc. Although it is true that few families are now economic units (although a growing number of people are self-employed and/or work from home), it has been argued that the family remains an important unit of consumption. Some of the most expensive items, for example houses and cars, are usually bought by families. Leisure, too, is increasingly packaged as a family commodity, and many leisure pursuits are still carried out within the family.

Further empirical evidence against the view expressed in Item B.

Parsons, a functionalist, argued that even though the modern family had lost many of the functions it used to perform, it had actually become more specialised, and its remaining functions were still vital for society.

An important point showing a functionalist response to the changing functions of the family.

The majority of people spend most of their life as part of a family, so how is it possible to say that the family has been stripped of its functions? 'Significant' is another way of saying 'important', and the evidence shows it isn't true that the family is no longer important as a social institution. What could be said, though, is that the family and its functions have changed, but it is still one of the most significant social institutions that we have.

A good, brief conclusion which arises logically from the arguments presented in the body of the answer.

Overall this is a well-focused and well-argued answer, showing good evidence of the skills, especially analysis and evaluation, which carry the bulk of the marks for this question. Good sociological knowledge and understanding are shown throughout, for 17 marks out of 20.

Social policies on the family; marriage; childhood

Item A

Many people have drawn attention to the improvements that have been made over the last 100 years in the quality of family life for people in Britain. Others point out that while in many respects life has indeed got better, the modern isolated nuclear family faces many problems. For many people, family life is a constant struggle against low income, poor housing, ill health and a lack of amenities such as nearby shops, good schools, reliable public transport and safe places for children to play. Even for those with better material resources, family life can also bring stress. For many couples, juggling the demands of work, home and childcare, with no kin nearby to help, life seems a perpetual struggle. For lone parents, such problems are often multiplied.

Concern over the decline in the traditional nuclear family and so-called 'traditional family values' has led the government to focus on ways of strengthening the family unit, including the introduction of so-called 'family-friendly' policies.

Item B

Ariès claimed that childhood did not exist in medieval times. Attitudes towards children were changing, in the upper levels of society at least, by the seventeenth century. However, childhood, as people think of it today, did not become clearly established for the mass of the population until the nineteenth century, when changes occurred that created a space for childhood between infancy and adulthood and kept children in the parental home for a longer period.

Recent changes have to some extent undermined the distinctiveness of child-hood. Television's penetration into the household has given children a virtually unrestricted access to the adult world. Children have also become increasingly treated as individuals in their own right. Thus, the Children's Act of 1989 made changes in their legal status, treating them less as minors without rights and more as individuals, with the right to have their wishes and feelings taken into account by, for example, the courts or those running children's homes.

Source: adapted from Fulcher and Scott (1999) *Sociology*, Oxford University Press.

(a) **Explain what is meant by the 'isolated nuclear family' (Item A).**   (2 marks)

(b) **Identify** *two* **'traditional family values' which some people believe have declined in recent years.**   (4 marks)

(c) **Suggest** *three* **ways in which the quality of family life has improved over the last 100 years.**   (6 marks)

(d) Identify and briefly explain **two** social policies designed to strengthen the family unit. (8 marks)

(e) Examine the sociological reasons for the decline in the popularity of marriage over the last 30 years. (20 marks)

(f) Using material from Item B and elsewhere, assess the view that the 'distinctiveness of childhood' has been undermined. (20 marks)

Total: 60 marks

■ ■ ■

Task This question is for you to try yourself. You should spend some time researching suitable material and making notes, and then try to write the answer in 75 minutes — the time you will be allowed in the examination. Below are a few pointers to try to make sure that you are on the right track.

(a) It would be wise here to show that you understand both parts of the concept, i.e. 'nuclear' and 'isolated'.

(b) Think carefully about this — the question is not about simple 'changes in the family', but changes in 'family values'. Make sure that your answer clearly refers to 'values'.

(c) While it is, of course, true that not all social groups have experienced equal improvements in the quality of family life, there are some improvements from which most people have benefited. You might think about health, housing, childbirth, working hours and laws designed to protect children, for example.

(d) Many such social policies have been introduced, particularly in the last few years. If you are not confident about your knowledge of social policies, try checking on the official government website (**www.open.gov.uk**), looking under 'Families'. Such knowledge is important, and you should have an awareness of current social policies in all the topic areas you are studying.

(e) In a question such as this, it is often a good idea to start by describing the situation. In this case, it would mean giving some information regarding the decline in marriage from the early 1970s (always check to see whether there is a specific time-scale mentioned in the question). It would also be relevant to mention cohabitation and some significant features regarding the marriages that do take place, for example the proportion of remarriages, and the growing trend towards civil, rather than religious, ceremonies. However, do not spend long on these aspects, and show how they are relevant to your discussion. The main part of the answer will be on the sociological (as opposed to common-sense) explanations of this trend. You might find references to feminist and postmodern views helpful here.

(f) You need to read Item B carefully, as there is a lot of information which will help you to identify what it was that might have been thought to make childhood 'distinctive'. You should then examine some of the changes that have taken place. However, remember that this is the question carrying most marks for the skills, including evaluation, so you should also take a critical look at the evidence. This could mean examining the extent to which childhood actually was 'distinctive' in the past, as well as whether the changes referred to have actually undermined the distinctive nature of childhood. In other words, you are presenting evidence both for and against the positions, and then trying to make a judgement.